# GCSE Maths AQA Practice Paper Questions
# Higher
# Grade 9 – 1 Course

Barton Maths Tuition

**GCSE Maths AQA Practice Paper Questions Higher 9 – 1 Course**

This book contains two complete sets of practice paper questions.

Full written solutions are provided for every question.

The questions are highly realistic and accurately match the AQA specification.

Paper 1 is a non-calculator paper and Papers 2 and 3 are calculator papers.

Allow 90 minutes to complete each paper.

# CONTENTS

# ACKNOWLEDGMENTS

The author wishes to thank Julia Sands for providing the illustrations and for editing this book.

# Paper 1 Higher: Practice Set 1

**1**

Simplify $2^6 \times 2^8$

Circle your answer.

$4^{14}$        $2^{14}$        $2^{48}$        $4^{48}$

**2**

Give a reason why these two triangles are congruent.    SAS

4cm     35°     5cm

35°   4cm   5cm

**3**

Which of the following is a geometric progression?

Circle your answer.

3,    6,    9,    12,    15          5,    10,    20,    40,    80

13,    9,    5,    1,    −3          3,    6,    9,    13,    17

**4**

$x : y = 2 : 5$

Circle the correct statement.

$x$ is $\frac{2}{5}$ of $y$      $y$ is $\frac{2}{5}$ of $x$      $x$ is $\frac{2}{7}$ of $y$      $y$ is $\frac{2}{7}$ of $x$

**5**

Write 72 as a product of prime factors.

Give your answer in index form.

$2^3 \times 3^2$

**6**

The table shows the times taken by 12 people to complete a crossword.

| Time $t$ minutes | Frequency |
|---|---|
| $10 < t \le 20$ | 5 |
| $20 < t \le 30$ | 2 |
| $30 < t \le 40$ | 5 |

**(a)**

Find the lower and upper bounds for the mean.

**(b)**

Find the lower and upper bounds for the range.

1

**7**

$\frac{4}{5}$ of a number is 340.

What is the number?

*(handwritten working:* $5\overline{)340}$ = 068, $68 \times 4 = 272$*)*

**8**

$x$ pounds $= y$ kilograms.

Use 11 pounds = 5 kilograms to write a formula for $y$ in terms of $x$.   $11x = 5y$

**9**

$$\text{pressure} = \frac{\text{force}}{\text{area}}$$

$P = \frac{8Q}{2Q} = 4$

The force exerted by shape $P$ is 8 times the force exerted by shape $Q$.
The area in contact with the ground of shape $P$ is 2 times the area of shape $Q$.
How many times greater is the pressure exerted by shape $P$ than shape $Q$?   $4 \times$ ✗

**10**

$$\text{current} = \frac{\text{voltage}}{\text{resistance}}$$

If the voltage is 4 times greater and the resistance is halved, what happens to the current?   $8\times$

**11**

Solve these simultaneous equations:

$3x + 2y = 26$

$x - 2y = -18$

*(handwritten working:* $4x = 8$, $x = 2$; $2 - 2y = -18$, $-2y = -20$, $-y = -10$, $y = 10$*)*

**12**

Tickets for an air display are on sale.
Tickets cost £50.
There is a 10% booking fee.
5% is then added if the ticket is bought within a week of the air display.
A man buys a ticket 4 days before the air display.
How much does he pay?

*(handwritten working:* 10% of £50 = £5, 110% = £55, 5% of £55 = £2.75, 55+2.75=£57.75*)*

£ 57.75

**13**

The sides of the square form 4 tangents to the circle.
The area of the circle is $81\pi$ cm$^2$.
Find the area of the square.

*(handwritten working:* $\pi r^2$, $r^2 = 81$ cm, $r = 9$ cm, $d = 18$ cm, $18^2 = 324$ cm$^2$*)*

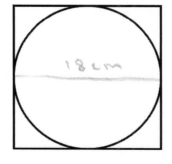

18 cm

**14**

Write the number three hundred million ten thousand in standard form.

**15**
Solve $-4x \geq 12$

$-x \geq 3$

$x \leq -3$

**16**
Which of these four fractions converts to a recurring decimal?
Circle any answers.

$\frac{4}{12} = \frac{1}{3}$      $\frac{12}{30} = \frac{4}{10}$      $\frac{1}{8}$      $\frac{100}{31} = 3\frac{7}{31}$

**17**
Some information on the marks of 80 students in a maths test are shown.

| Mark $m$ | Frequency | cF |
|---|---|---|
| $30 < m \leq 40$ | 13 | 13 |
| $40 < m \leq 50$ | 24 | 37 |
| $50 < m \leq 60$ | 27 | 64 |
| $60 < m \leq 80$ | 12 | 76 |
| $80 < m \leq 100$ | 4 | 80 |

**(a)**
Draw a cumulative frequency graph for the data on the graph below.

**(b)**
Estimate the lowest mark of the top 10% of students.

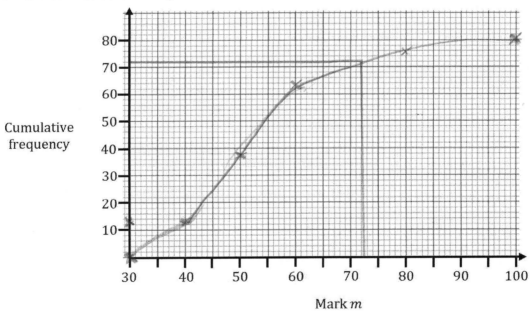

Cumulative frequency

Mark $m$

**18**
Work out the diameter of the circle $x^2 + y^2 = 81$

$x^2 + y^2 = r^2 = 81$

$r = 9$

$2r = d = 18$

18

**19**
$P$ is the point $(5, -8)$
$Q$ is the point $(-10, 16)$
Find the equation of the straight line passing through $P$ and $Q$.

15

24

**20**

A line has equation $y = -2x + 108$

Does the point $(-104, 316)$ lie on this line? Explain your answer.    $-2(-104) + 108 = 316$

**21**

Three shops sell the same bread rolls at the same price.

Each shop has a different offer.    roll = x

| **Shop A** | **Shop B** | **Shop C** |
|---|---|---|
| Buy 2 rolls and get the third free | Buy 3 rolls and get 2 free | 20% off each roll |

$2x + x$          $3x + 2x$          $\frac{4x}{5}$

What is the cheapest way of buying 12 rolls?

**22**

A fair octahedral dice has eight faces numbered 1 to 8.    2,3,5,7

A fair six-sided spinner has five blue faces and one yellow face.

The dice is rolled.

If the dice shows a prime number, the spinner is spun.

Draw a probability tree for the dice and the spinner.

Label all the branches.

**23**

A fair six-sided dice has two red faces and four green faces.

The dice is rolled three times.

What is the probability of getting no red faces?

**24**

Find three different single transformations that map rectangle A to rectangle B.

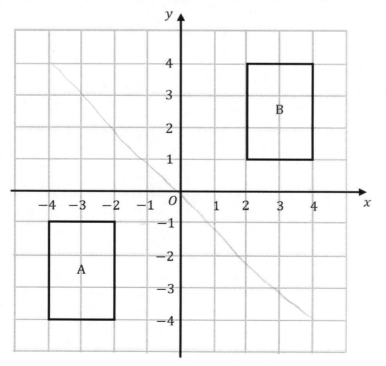

enlargement sf -1 center O

translation $\binom{6}{5}$

reflection in $y = -x$

**25**
Triangle A is mapped to triangle B by two single transformations.
The first is a rotation 90° anticlockwise about the point $(-3, -2)$
Describe fully the second transformation.

enlargement sf -2
center (1,-1)

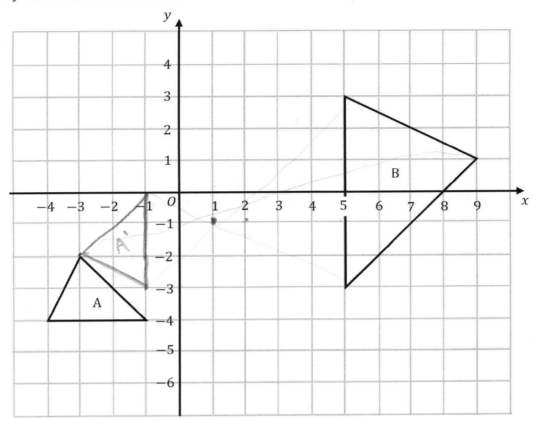

**26**
$ABC$ and $ADE$ are similar triangles.
$DE$ and $BC$ are parallel.

Write another fraction equivalent to $\dfrac{BC}{DE}$   $\dfrac{AC}{AE}$

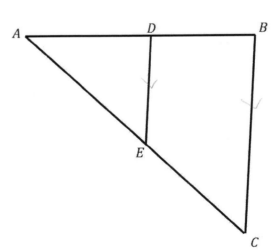

**27**

Work out $\sqrt{5\dfrac{1}{16}}$ as a mixed number.

$16 \times 5 = 80$

$\sqrt{\dfrac{81}{16}} = \dfrac{9}{4}$        $2\dfrac{1}{4}$

**28**

Here is a velocity-time graph.
Find the distance travelled in the last 20 seconds.   200m

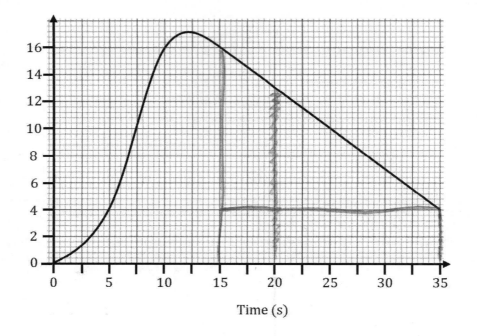

$$\frac{20 \times 12}{2} = 120m$$

$$20 \times 4 = 80$$

**29**

This is a velocity-time graph.
Find the times when the acceleration was zero.   15s, 30s

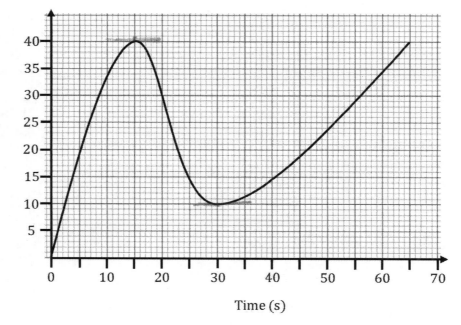

**30**

Work out $\sqrt[3]{32}$ as a power of 2.

$\sqrt[3]{2^5}$

$32 = 2 \times 2 \times 2 \times 2 \times 2$
$= 2^5$

$2^2$

**31**

At a company there are three times as many females as males.

$f = 3m$

$\frac{1}{6}$ of the females are part-time.

$\frac{f}{6} + \frac{2m}{5} = \frac{3m}{6} + \frac{2m}{5}$

$\frac{2}{5}$ of the males are part-time.

$\frac{m}{2} + \frac{2m}{5}$

126 people are part-time.

Find the number of people in the company.

$9m = 1260$
$m = 140$

$\frac{5m}{10} + \frac{4m}{10} = 126$

$140 \times 4 = 560$

**32**

Expand and simplify $(x-3)(4x+2y)^2$

$(x-3)(16x^2 + 8xy + 8xy + 4y^2) = (x-3)(16x^2 + 16xy + 64y^2)$
$16x^3 + 16x^2 y + 4xy^2$

**33**

$A(2,3)$ is a point on the circle centre $O$.
Work out the equation of the tangent to the circle at $A$.
Give your answer in the form $y = mx + c$

$\frac{3-2}{3} - \sqrt{3}$

gradient of $r = \frac{3}{2}$

$-\frac{2}{3}$

$\frac{1}{\sqrt{13}} \times \frac{\sqrt{13}}{\sqrt{13}} \times \frac{\sqrt{13}}{13}$

$3 = \frac{\sqrt{13}}{13}$

$y = -\frac{2}{3}x + c$

$3 = -\frac{2}{3}(2) + c$

$3 = -\frac{4}{3} + c$

$\frac{13}{3} = c$

$y = -\frac{2}{3}x + \frac{13}{3}$

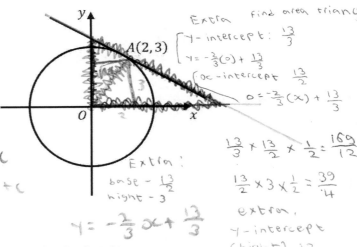

Extra  find area triangle

y-intercept: $\frac{13}{3}$

$y = -\frac{2}{3}(0) + \frac{13}{3}$

x-intercept $\frac{13}{2}$

$0 = -\frac{2}{3}(x) + \frac{13}{3}$

$\frac{13}{3} \times \frac{13}{2} \times \frac{1}{2} = \frac{169}{12}$

$\frac{13}{2} \times 3 \times \frac{1}{2} = \frac{39}{4}$

Extra:
base - $\frac{13}{2}$
hight - 3

extra,
y-intercept
(hight) $\frac{13}{3}$

$\frac{1}{2} \times \frac{13}{3} \times 2 = \frac{13}{3}$

**34**

volume of cone $= \frac{1}{3}\pi r^2 h$ where $r$ is the radius and $h$ is the perpendicular height.

A cone of height 25cm and radius 10cm is partially filled with water.
The cone contains water to a depth of 15cm.
Work out the volume of the water, in cm³.
Give your answer in terms of $\pi$.

$\frac{1}{3}\pi \times 6^2 \times 10 = 500\pi$

$\frac{2500\pi}{3} - 500 = \frac{1000\pi}{3}$

$\frac{1}{3}\pi 10^2 \times 25$

$= \frac{2500}{3}\pi$

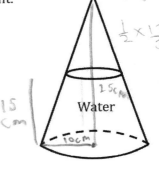

15 cm
Water
10cm
25cm

**35**

Simplify

$\frac{3\tan 60° - \sin 60°}{4\cos 45}$

Give your answer in the form $k\sqrt{6}$ where $k$ is a constant.

$\frac{3(\sqrt{3}) - (\frac{\sqrt{3}}{2})}{4(\frac{1}{\sqrt{2}})} = \frac{3 - \sqrt{3} - \frac{\sqrt{3}}{2}}{2\sqrt{2}}$

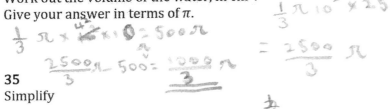

$3\sqrt{3} - \frac{\sqrt{3}}{2}$

$\frac{6\sqrt{3}}{2} - \frac{\sqrt{3}}{2} = \frac{5\sqrt{3}}{2}$

$\frac{\left(\frac{5\sqrt{3}}{2}\right)}{2\sqrt{2}} = \frac{5\sqrt{3}}{2 \times 2\sqrt{2}}$

$\frac{5\sqrt{3}}{4\sqrt{2}}$

$\frac{5\sqrt{3}}{4\sqrt{2}} \times \frac{\sqrt{2}}{\sqrt{2}} = \frac{5\sqrt{6}}{8}$

$\frac{5}{8}\sqrt{6}$

$k = \frac{5}{8}$

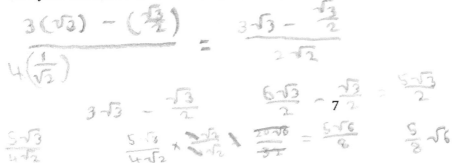

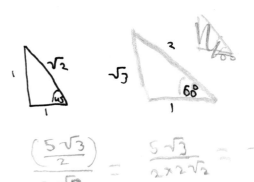

## Paper 1 Higher: Practice Set 1 Solutions

**1**

Using the law of indices,
$$a^m \times a^n = a^{m+n}$$
so
$$2^6 \times 2^8 = 2^{14}$$

**2**

The triangles are congruent due to side-angle-side (SAS).
This is recognised as the angle sandwich formed by 4cm, 35°, 5cm.

**3**

In a geometric progression, each term is multiplied (or divided) by the same amount to get to the next term.
This is true of the sequence $5, 10, 20, 40, 80$, since each term is two times the previous term.

**4**

$x : y = 2 : 5$
You can cross-multiply to form an equation: $5x = 2y$
So $x = \frac{2}{5}y$ therefore $x$ is $\frac{2}{5}$ of $y$ is the correct answer.

Cross-multiplying a ratio

$x : y$

$2 : 5$

$5x = 2y$

**5**

$$72 = 2 \times 2 \times 2 \times 3 \times 3$$
$$= 2^3 \times 3^2$$

**6(a)**

Use the lower values in the time ranges to get the lower bound of the mean:
$$\frac{10 \times 5 + 20 \times 2 + 30 \times 5}{12} = 20$$
Use the upper values in the time ranges to get the upper bound of the mean:
$$\frac{20 \times 5 + 30 \times 2 + 40 \times 5}{12} = 30$$
The lower bound of the mean is 20 and the upper bound of the mean is 30.
$20 < \text{mean} \leq 30$
Note the mean cannot be 20 since the lower values in the inequalities were excluded.

**6(b)**

The upper bound for the range is found by taking the shortest possible time away from the longest amount of time as shown: $40 - 10 = 30$

| Time $t$ minutes | Frequency |
|---|---|
| ⑩$< t \leq 20$ | 5 |
| $20 < t \leq 30$ | 2 |
| $30 < t \leq$ ㊵ | 5 |

The lower bound for the range is found by taking the larger value from the first interval from the smaller value from the last interval as shown: $30 - 20 = 10$

| Time $t$ minutes | Frequency |
|---|---|
| $10 < t \leq$ ⑳ | 5 |
| $20 < t \leq 30$ | 2 |
| ㉚$< t \leq 40$ | 5 |

The lower bound of the range is 10 and the upper bound of the range is 30.

**7**

Let the number be $x$:

"$\frac{4}{5}$ of" means "$\frac{4}{5} \times$" so

$\frac{4}{5} \times x = 340$

$x = 340 \times \dfrac{5}{4}$

$\quad = 425$

Divide by 4, then multiply by 5:

$$4 \overline{\smash{)}3\,^3 4\,^2 0} \quad\quad \begin{array}{r} 8\ \ 5 \\ \times \quad\ 5 \\ \hline 4\ \ 2\ \ 5 \\ \ \ 2 \end{array}$$

$\phantom{4}\quad 8\ \ 5$

**8**

$x : y = 11 : 5$

Cross-multiply to give $5x = 11y$

So $y = \dfrac{5}{11}x$

Cross-multiplying a ratio

$x : y$

$11 : 5$

$5x = 11y$

**9**

Write the multiplier in front of each of the variables in the formula:

$$\text{pressure} = \frac{8 \times \text{force}}{2 \times \text{area}}$$

$$= 4 \times \frac{\text{force}}{\text{area}}$$

The overall multiplier is 4, so the pressure exerted by shape $P$ will be 4 times greater than that of shape $Q$.

**10**

Write the multiplier in front of the variable in the formula:

$$\text{current} = \frac{4 \times \text{voltage}}{0.5 \times \text{resistance}}$$

$$= \frac{4}{0.5} \times \frac{\text{voltage}}{\text{resistance}}$$

$$= 8 \times \frac{\text{voltage}}{\text{resistance}}$$

The overall multiplier is 8, so the current will be 8 times greater.

**11**

$3x + 2y = 26$

$\ x - 2y = -18$

Notice the number in front of $y$ in both equations is the same size and of opposite sign: 2 and $-2$

Add both equations:

$$\begin{array}{r} 3x + 2y = 26 \quad [1] \\ +\ \ x - 2y = -18 \quad [2] \\ \hline 4x = 8 \\ x = 2 \end{array}$$

Substitute $x = 2$ into either equation (using equation [1]):

$6 + 2y = 26$

$\quad 2y = 20$

$$y = 10$$
$$x = 2 \text{ and } y = 10$$

## 12

One ticket is bought which incurs the 10% booking fee.
10% of £50 is £5 (divide by 10).
The cost is currently £55.
5% is added since the ticket was bought 4 days before the display (question said 5% added if bought within a week of the air display).
5% of £55 is £2.75 (10% is £5.50, halving gives 5%).
Adding this gives a total payment of £57.75.

## 13

The diameter of the circle is equal to the side length of the square.
Use the area of the circle to find the radius, and then diameter:
$$\pi r^2 = 81\pi$$
$$r^2 = 81$$
$$r = 9$$
The diameter is 18cm.
Square the diameter (side length of the square) to get the area:
$$18^2 = 324$$
The area of the square is 324cm$^2$.

## 14

We word numbers as a sum of their components:
Three hundred million: 300,000,000
Ten thousand: 10,000
Combine them by adding: $300,000,000 + 10,000 = 300,010,000$
Now write in standard form:
The decimal must proceed the 3 to convert the numeric value to between 1 and 10:
The decimal has moved 8 places to the left to give an answer of
$3.0001 \times 10^8$

## 15

Solving an inequality requires the same techniques as that of solving an equation.
There are two scenarios where inequalities differ from equations:
If you multiply or divide by a negative number, or take reciprocals of both sides, the inequality sign is flipped.
$$-4x \geq 12$$
$$x \leq -3$$
The sign is flipped since both sides were divided by $-4$

## 16

Make sure all the fractions are fully simplified to give:

$$\frac{1}{3} \qquad \frac{2}{5} \qquad \frac{1}{8} \qquad \frac{100}{31}$$

Now write the denominators as a product of their primes.
Note that 3, 5 and 31 are primes so only 8 will change to $2^3$.
If the denominator contains any primes that are not 2 or 5 then it will recur.
Therefore, two of these fractions will recur:

$$\frac{4}{12} \text{ and } \frac{100}{31}$$

## 17(a)
Draw another column on the right labelled cumulative frequency.
Then plot the upper value of the mark inequality against the cumulative frequency value.
Note that no student scored less than 30 marks, so we also plot a point at $(30, 0)$

| Mark $m$ | Frequency | Cumulative frequency |
|---|---|---|
| $30 < m \leq 40$ | 13 | 13 |
| $40 < m \leq 50$ | 24 | 37 |
| $50 < m \leq 60$ | 27 | 64 |
| $60 < m \leq 80$ | 12 | 76 |
| $80 < m \leq 100$ | 4 | 80 |

Plot the points as shown below:

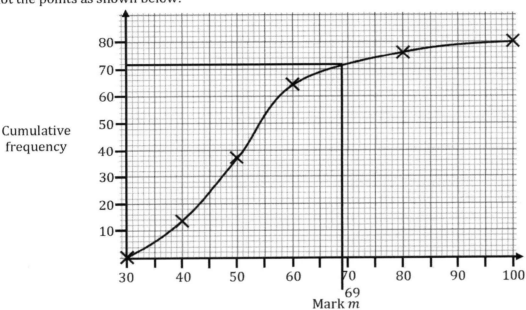

## 17(b)
The top 10% of students is the top 8 students, since 10% of 80 is 8.
Since it is the top values we are looking for, we subtract 8 from 80 to get 72.
Draw a horizontal line from 72 on the cumulative frequency axis until it intersects the curve.
Draw a vertical line from the intersection to the mark axis to get the answer.
There will be some variation depending on the graph drawn, but answers of $69 \pm 1$ will be acceptable.

## 18
The general equation of a circle with its centre at the origin is $x^2 + y^2 = r^2$
$r$ is the radius.
$x^2 + y^2 = 81 \Rightarrow r^2 = 81$
So $r = 9$
The diameter is twice the radius: $2 \times 9 = 18$
The diameter is 18.

**19**

The general equation of a straight line is $y = mx + c$
$m$ is the gradient and $c$ is the $y$-axis intercept.
Start with the gradient:

$$m = \frac{\text{difference in } y \text{ values}}{\text{difference in } x \text{ values}}$$

$$= \frac{-8 - 16}{5 - (-10)}$$

$$= -\frac{24}{15}$$

$$= -\frac{8}{5}$$

So far the equation is $y = -\frac{8}{5}x + c$

Substitute a coordinate pairing into the equation to find $c$, in this case $(5, -8)$:

$$-8 = -\frac{8}{5}(5) + c$$

$$-8 = -8 + c$$

$$c = 0$$

The equation of the line is $y = -\frac{8}{5}x$

**20**

If a point lies on a line, the value of $x$ can be substituted into the equation to give the value $y$.
If $-104$ is substituted into $y = -2x + 108$ and the value of $y$ generated is 316, then the point $(-104, 316)$ lies on the line.

$$y = -2(-104) + 108$$

$$= 208 + 108$$

$$= 316$$

Therefore, the point $(-104, 316)$ lies on the line.

**21**

The rolls are sold individually at the same price.
Let the price of each roll be £$x$ (you can pick any value as long as you are consistent).
Express the "pound for pound" price for each shop:
Shop A:
"Buy two rolls and get the third free" is the same as paying £$2x$ and getting 3 rolls:
3 rolls = £$2x$

1 roll = £$\frac{2}{3}x$

Shop B:
"Buy 3 rolls and get 2 free" is the same as paying £$3x$ and getting 5 rolls:
5 rolls = £$3x$

1 roll = £$\frac{3}{5}x$

Note that $\frac{3}{5}$ is less than $\frac{2}{3}$, so Shop B is cheaper so far.

Shop C:
"20% off each roll" is the same as paying £$0.8x$ and getting one roll:
1 roll = £$0.8x$

0.8 is greater than $\frac{2}{3}$ and $\frac{3}{5}$; however, you are buying on an individual basis rather than as part of a larger deal.
The cheapest way to buy 12 rolls is:
2 lots from Shop B, which would be 10 rolls.

2 lots from Shop C, which would be 2 rolls.
This gives 12 rolls altogether.
Although Shop A is cheaper per roll than Shop C, you purchase in units of 3 (at a price of £2$x$).
Buying two rolls from Shop C costs £1.6$x$, which makes it cheaper.

## 22

There are four prime numbers in the first 8 integers: 2, 3, 5 and 7.

The probability of rolling a prime number will be $\frac{1}{2}$.

The spinner is spun only if a prime is rolled.
The spinner branching will only be applicable if a prime number is rolled.
The correct tree diagram is shown below:

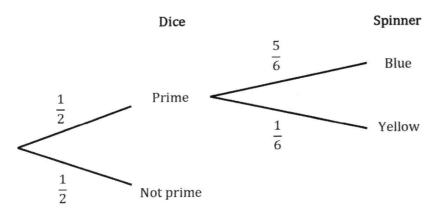

## 23

Probability of not rolling a red face $= \frac{4}{6}$, which is simplified to $\frac{2}{3}$.

Probability of not rolling a red three times in a row:

$$\left(\frac{2}{3}\right)^3 = \frac{8}{27}$$

## 24

These are the 3 possible transformations:

1. Rotation 180° centre the origin

2. Translation $\begin{pmatrix} 6 \\ 5 \end{pmatrix}$

3. Enlargement scale factor −1 centre the origin

## 25

Implement the first transformation as shown:
"rotation 90° anticlockwise about the point $(-3, -2)$"
The sides of the shape B are twice as long as those of the rotated triangle A.
This implies an enlargement of scale factor 2.
Triangle B is not orientated in the same direction as rotated triangle A.
This implies the enlargement is negative: −2.
Join the corners of rotated triangle A to the corresponding corners of triangle B.
Where the lines cross is the centre of the enlargement: $(1, -1)$
The second transformation is:
Enlargement scale factor −2 centre $(1, -1)$

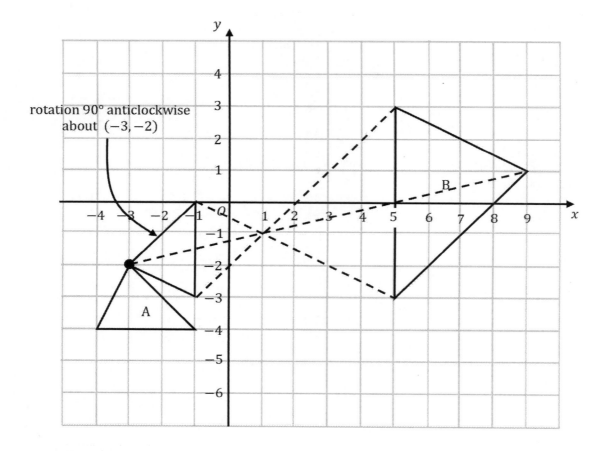

rotation 90° anticlockwise about $(-3, -2)$

**26**

If two triangles are similar, the ratio of corresponding sides are equal.

There are two possible answers: $\frac{AB}{AD}$ or $\frac{AC}{AE}$

Note that the given fraction $\frac{BC}{DE}$ had the side from the larger triangle ($ABC$) on the numerator and the side from the smaller triangle ($ADE$) on the denominator.

This ordering must be maintained in the answer.

**27**

$$\sqrt{5\frac{1}{16}} = \sqrt{\frac{81}{16}}$$

$$= \frac{9}{4}$$

$$= 2\frac{1}{4}$$

**28**

The distance travelled is given by finding the area under the velocity-time graph for the last 20 seconds.

This is from 15 to 35 seconds.

The area can be split into a triangle and a rectangle (or a trapezium).

Area of rectangle $= 4 \times 20$

$= 80$

Area of triangle $= \frac{1}{2} \times 20 \times 12$

$= 120$
Total area is $80 + 120 = 200$ metres
Distance travelled was 200m.

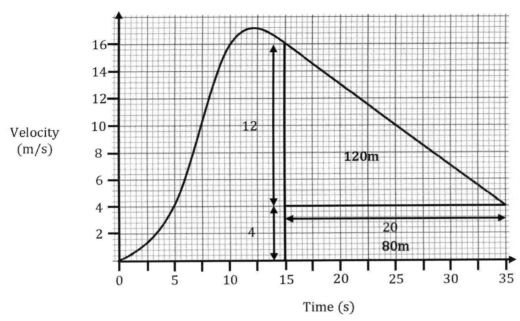

## 29

The acceleration is given by the gradient of the velocity-time graph.
The acceleration will be zero when the gradient is zero (horizontal).
This happens at two times:
Around 15s and around 30s.

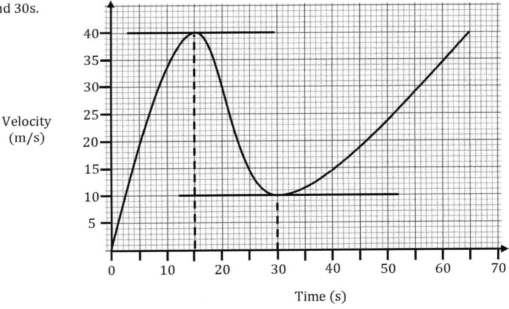

## 30

The cube root as a power is $\frac{1}{3}$.

32 as a power of 2 is $2^5$.

Using the law of indices: $(a^m)^n = a^{mn}$

$$\sqrt[3]{32} = (2^5)^{\frac{1}{3}}$$
$$= 2^{\frac{5}{3}}$$

**31**

Call the number of males at the company $x$.

There will be $3x$ females at the company.

$\frac{1}{6}$ of $3x$ are part-time females: $\frac{1}{6} \times 3x = \frac{1}{2}x$

$\frac{2}{5}$ of $x$ are part-time males: $\frac{2}{5} \times x = \frac{2}{5}x$

The total number of part-time employees is 126:

$$\frac{1}{2}x + \frac{2}{5}x = 126$$
$$\frac{9}{10}x = 126$$
$$x = 140$$

$$\frac{1}{2} + \frac{2}{5} = \frac{5}{10} + \frac{4}{10}$$
$$= \frac{9}{10}$$

Divide by 9, then multiply by 10:

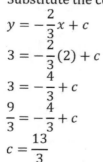

The total number of people in the company is $3x + x = 4x$

$$4x = 4 \times 140$$
$$= 560$$

There are 560 people in the company.

**32**

$$(x - 3)(4x + 2y)^2 = (x - 3)(4x + 2y)(4x + 2y)$$
$$= (x - 3)(16x^2 + 8xy + 8xy + 4y^2)$$
$$= (x - 3)(16x^2 + 16xy + 4y^2)$$
$$= 16x^3 + 16x^2y + 4xy^2 - 48x^2 - 48xy - 12y^2$$

**33**

The tangent will be perpendicular to the gradient of the radius from the origin to point $A$.

The gradient of the radius will be $\frac{3}{2}$.

The gradient of the tangent will be the negative reciprocal of the gradient of the radius: $-\frac{2}{3}$

The tangent is a straight line with general equation $y = mx + c$

$m = -\frac{2}{3}$ as this represents the gradient.

Substitute the coordinates of $A$ into the line equation to find the value of $c$:

$$y = -\frac{2}{3}x + c$$
$$3 = -\frac{2}{3}(2) + c$$
$$3 = -\frac{4}{3} + c$$
$$\frac{9}{3} = -\frac{4}{3} + c$$
$$c = \frac{13}{3}$$

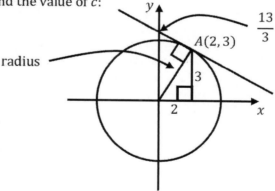

The equation of the tangent is $y = -\frac{2}{3}x + \frac{13}{3}$

**34**

The water depth is 15cm, so the remaining height above the water level is 10cm.

The empty volume above the water level is a cone similar to the large cone.

The water volume is the difference between the volumes of the large and small cones.

Since the small cone has a height of 10cm and the large cone 25cm, we can calculate the ratio of the heights: $\frac{10}{25} = \frac{2}{5}$, so the small cone lengths are all $\frac{2}{5}$ of the large cone.

16

The small cone radius is $\frac{2}{5} \times 10 = 4$ cm

The water volume is:

$$\frac{1}{3}\pi \times 10^2 \times 25 - \frac{1}{3}\pi \times 4^2 \times 10 = \frac{1}{3}\pi \times 100 \times 25 - \frac{1}{3}\pi \times 16 \times 10$$
$$= \frac{2500}{3}\pi - \frac{160}{3}\pi$$
$$= 780\pi$$

The volume of water is $780\pi\,\mathrm{cm}^3$.

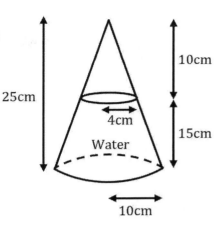

**35**

$\tan 60° = \sqrt{3}$

$\sin 60° = \dfrac{\sqrt{3}}{2}$

$\cos 45° = \dfrac{\sqrt{2}}{2}$

$$\frac{3\tan 60° - \sin 60°}{4\cos 45} = \frac{3 \times \sqrt{3} - \frac{\sqrt{3}}{2}}{4 \times \frac{\sqrt{2}}{2}}$$
$$= \frac{3\sqrt{3} - \frac{\sqrt{3}}{2}}{2\sqrt{2}}$$
$$= \frac{6\sqrt{3} - \sqrt{3}}{4\sqrt{2}}$$
$$= \frac{5\sqrt{3}}{4\sqrt{2}}$$
$$= \frac{5\sqrt{3}}{4\sqrt{2}} \times \frac{\sqrt{2}}{\sqrt{2}}$$
$$= \frac{5\sqrt{6}}{8}$$

$k = \dfrac{5}{8}$

## Paper 2 Higher: Practice Set 1

**1**

Circle the decimal closest in value to $\frac{73}{1600}$

    0.04565      0.0456      0.046      (0.04563)

**2**

Convert 48mm$^2$ into m$^2$.
Circle the correct area.

    0.048m$^2$      0.0048m$^2$      0.00048m$^2$      (0.000048m$^2$)

**3**

Circle the midpoint of $A(3, 8)$ and $B(-7, 16)$

    $(5, 12)$      $(-4, 8)$      $(-2, 12)$      $(10, 8)$

**4**

Circle the formula for the $n$th term for the sequence.

102      96      90      84      78

Circle your answer:

    $-6n - 108$      $(108 - 6n)$      $6n + 108$      $6n - 108$

**5**

A padlock uses a four-digit code.
Each digit can take any value from 0 to 9.
Digits can be repeated.
The first three digits are known.
The last digit is known to be a prime number.
What is the probability of correctly guessing the last digit?

**6**

A pin number uses a four-digit code.
Each digit can take any value from 0 to 9.
Digits can be repeated.
The first digit is 4.
The code is an odd number.
How many possible codes are there?

**7(a)**

Complete the table of values for $y = x^2 - 2x - 3$

| $x$ | $-3$ | $-1$ | 1 | 3 | 5 | 7 |
|---|---|---|---|---|---|---|
| $y$ | 12 | 0 | -4 | 0 | 12 | 32 |

**7(b)**
Draw the graph of $y = x^2 - 2x - 3$ for $-3 \leq x \leq 7$

**7(c)**
Find the coordinates of the turning point of the graph.

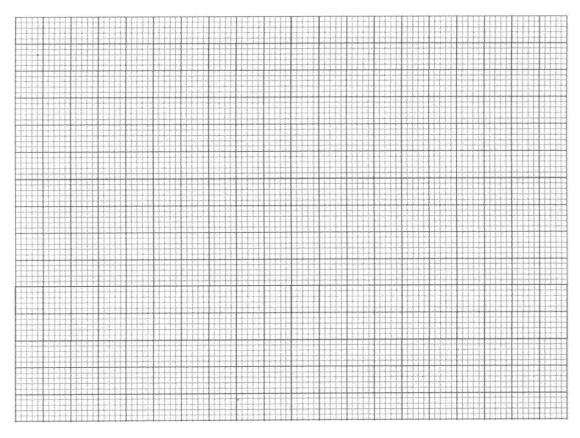

**8**
Use trigonometry to work out the length $a$.

7.3724

$\sin(55) \times 9$

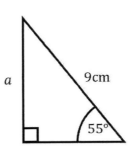

$a$    9cm

55°

**9(a)**
A car journey is described as follows:
For the first 40 minutes the average speed was 60mph.
The car stopped for 15 minutes.
The journey was completed at 56mph.
The total journey time is 85 minutes.
Find the average speed for the journey.

$\frac{55}{85}$    $\frac{20}{85} \times 56$

**9(b)**

A car journey is described as follows:

For the first 20 minutes the average speed was 60mph.

The car stopped for 10 minutes.

The journey was completed at 50mph.

The total journey time is 90 minutes.

Complete the distance-time graph for the journey. *70 miles*

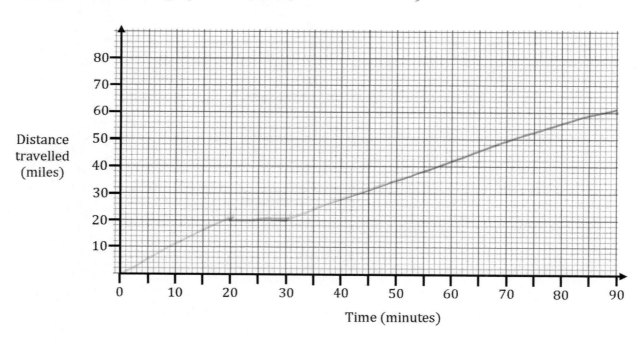

**10**

The number of each type of house in a village is shown in the table below.

| Type of house | Detached | Semi-detached | Terraced | Bungalow |
|---|---|---|---|---|
| Number | $2x + 9$ | $4x$ | 28 | $13x + 8$ |

*19x + 17*

A house is chosen at random.

The probability that it is terraced is $\frac{1}{5}$.

Work out the probability that it is a bungalow.

**11**

The pie chart shows information about an allotment.

There were 1204 more vegetables than fruit.

Work out the total number of fruit and vegetables.

$360 - 137 = 223$

$223 - 137 = 86$

$86 = 1204$

$360 / 86 = \frac{180}{43}$

$\frac{180}{43} \times 1204 = 5040$

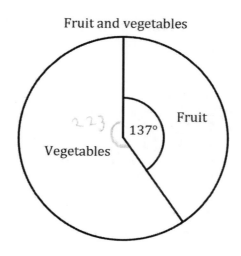

Fruit and vegetables

*223* 137° Fruit

Vegetables

20

**12**

Write these numbers in descending order:

4753        $4.75 \times 10^3$        $4.7 \times 2^{10}$        $4.5 \times 3^6$

*(handwritten: 2 over the first, marks 3, 4; 2 above third; 1 above fourth; 3 below second)*

**13**

$A, B$ and $C$ are points on a circle.

Prove $BC$ is a diameter.

*(handwritten: $180 - 35 - 55 = 90$, angle in semi-circle is $90°$)*

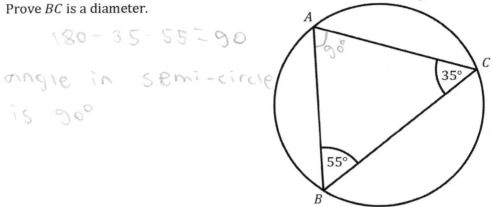

**14**

A cake requires 6 eggs and 1 packet of flour.

The eggs come in boxes of 15 priced at £2.56 per box.

The packets of flour cost £1.20 each and there is an offer of 3 for the price of 2.

A café is going to make some cakes.

There must be at least 109 cakes.

Work out the least amount that this would cost.

*(handwritten: $\frac{109 \times 6}{15} = 43.5$;   $44 \times 2.56 = £112.64$;   $3 \times 36 = 108$;   $72 \times 1.2 = £86.40$;   $86.4 + 1.2 + 112.64 = £200.24$)*

**15**

The graph shows the cost £$C$ of hiring a digger for $d$ days.

Work out a formula for the cost $C$ in terms of the number of days $d$.

*(handwritten: $C = 50d + 140$; 240; 140)*

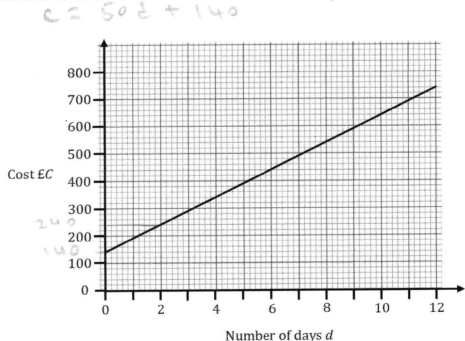

Number of days $d$

**X** **16(a)**

A student is using Pythagoras to find the value of $x$.
Here is the working:

$$a^2 + b^2 = c^2$$
$$x^2 + (x+1)^2 = (x+2)^2$$
$$x^2 + x^2 + 1 = x^2 + 4$$
$$2x^2 + 1 = x^2 + 4$$
$$x^2 + 1 = 4$$
$$x^2 = 3$$
$$x = \sqrt{3}$$

Correct any mistakes and find the solution.

*(handwritten)*
$x^2 + (x+1)^2 = (x+2)^2$
$x^2 + x^2 + 2x + 1 = x^2 + 4x + 4$
$2x^2 + 2x + 1 = x^2 + 4x + 4$
$x^2 - 2x = 3$
$y + 4 = 13$

$x^2 - 2x \cancel{5} - 3 = 0$
$(x-3)(x+1) = 0$
$x = \cancel{-1} \text{ or } 3$
$x$ is length

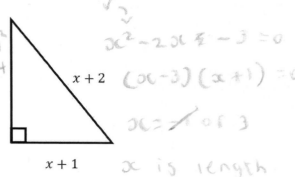

**16(b)**

Prove that the triangles shown are similar.

*(handwritten)* $x = 3$    sides in same ratio

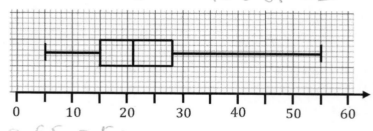

*(handwritten near right triangle)*
$(y+2)^2 + y^2 = (y+4)^2$
$y^2 + 4y + 4 + y^2 = y^2 + 8y + 16$
$2y^2 + 4y + 4 = y^2 + 8y + 16$
$y^2 - 4y - 12 = 0$
$(y-6)(y+2) = 0$
$y = 6 \text{ or } \cancel{-2}$

**17**

Here is a box plot.
Find the median value.

*(handwritten)* 21

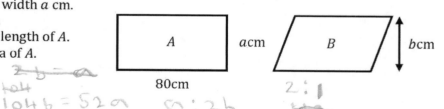

**18**

*(handwritten)* area B = $\cancel{8}$ · $80 \times 0.65 = 52a$

$A$ is a rectangle with length 80cm and width $a$ cm.
$B$ is a parallelogram with height $b$ cm.
The length of $B$ is 30% more than the length of $A$.
The area of $B$ is 35% less than the area of $A$.
Find the ratio $a : b$

*(handwritten)* $B = 80 \times 1.3 = 104$
$104 b$
$104 b = 52a$
$\cancel{\frac{2b}{a}} = \cancel{a}$
$a : 2b$
$2 : 1$

**19(a)**

A country club has 112 members.
70 are male and 42 are female.
$\frac{1}{2}$ of the male members are members of the gym.
$\frac{1}{3}$ of the female members are members of the gym.
$\xi$ = members of the country club
$M$ = male members
$G$ = members of the gym
Complete the Venn diagram.

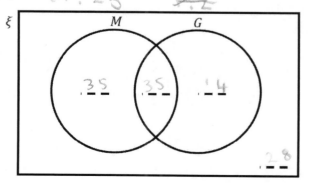

**19(b)**

$\xi$ = members of a wildlife trust
$M$ = male members
$T$ = members for more than 10 years
A member is chosen at random.
Given the member is male, find the probability that they have been a member for less than 10 years.

*(handwritten)*
348 + 152
= 500

348
───
500

M   T   ξ
348   152   184
86

**20**

A shop sells 325 bags of compost in the ratio small : medium : large = 4 : 9 : 12
The volume of one medium bag is twice the volume of one small bag.
The volume of one large bag is five times the volume of one small bag.
The total volume of compost is 21320 litres.
Work out the volume of one medium bag of compost.

*(handwritten)*
4S : 18S : 60S    82S
m = 2S
L = 5S
325 × 82 = 26650
21320/26650 = 4/5 = 0.8
0.8 × 2
= 1.6L    40L

**21**

Work out the size of angle $x$.

15cm

$x$   100°   7cm

*(handwritten)*
20. 4 + 9 + 12 = 25
325/25 = 13
52 : 117 : 156
52S + 234S + 780S = 1066S
21320/1066 = 20 = S

$\dfrac{\sin x}{7} = \dfrac{\sin 100}{15}$

$x = \sin^{-1}\left(\dfrac{\sin(100) \times 7}{15}\right)$

= 27.36°  2dp

**22**

Solve $4x^2 = 13x + 7$, giving your answers to 3 significant figures.

*(handwritten)*
$4x^2 - 13x - 7 = 0$

$\dfrac{13 \pm \sqrt{(-13)^2 - 4 \times (-7) \times 4}}{2 \times 4}$

= 3.72  or  -0.47

**23**

The volume of a cylinder $V$ cm³ is directly proportional to the square of the radius $r$ cm.
A cylinder of radius 5cm has a volume of 150cm³.
By what value will the volume increase when the radius increases to 7cm?

*(handwritten)*
r = 5   S² = 25   150/25 = 6
7² = 49   49 × 6 = 294 cm³

**24**

Prove $QRS$ is a straight line.

$6a - 2b$

P   S
$-2a + 5b$
$2a + 8b$
R
Q

*(handwritten)*
QR = 4a + 3b
QS = 8a + 6b
= 2(4a + 3b)
scalar multiples

$\frac{53}{2} = 26.5 = \text{median}$

$\frac{F}{FD \ CW}$

**25**

The histogram shows the results from 52 people who were asked to complete a sudoku.

37.916 –

13.125 =

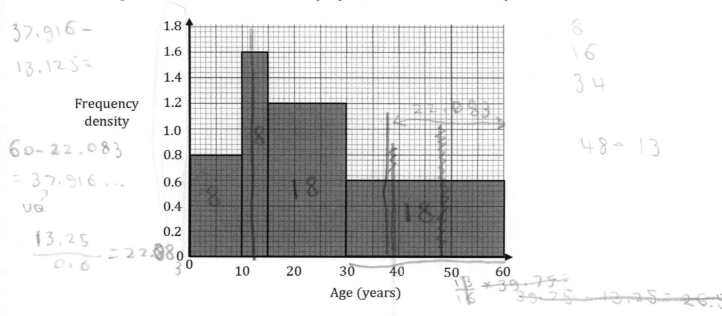

Frequency density

60 – 22.083

= 37.916 ...

UQ

$\frac{13.25}{0.6} = 22.08$

8

16

34

48 – 13

$\frac{13}{16} \times 39.75 =$

39.25 – 13.25 = 26.5

Work out an estimate for the interquartile range.

26.5  24.63

**26**

$\left[ \frac{53}{4} = 13.25 \qquad \frac{53 \times 3}{4} = 39.75 \right]$

A shape is formed from an equilateral triangle of side length 6cm and three semicircles.
Show that the area of the shape is 58.0cm² correct to 3 significant figures.

$\left( \frac{1}{2} \cos \sin A \times b \times c \right) + 3 \left( \frac{3^2 \times \pi}{2} \right)$

$\frac{1}{2} \sin(60) \times 6 \times 6 \qquad + \frac{27\pi}{2} = \frac{27\pi}{2}$

$= 57.999$

$= 58 \text{ cm}^3$

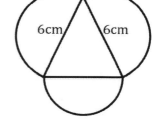

6cm  6cm

**27(a)**

A trapezium is shown below.

The trapezium is to be enlarged, scale factor $\frac{1}{2}$

If one point remains invariant, what does this tell you about the centre of enlargement?

it is on one
of the points

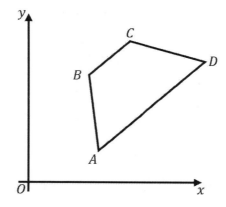

**27(b)**
A quadrilateral is shown below.
The points $P$ and $Q$ are invariant under a single transformation.
Describe the transformation.

a reflection

in $y = -x + 4$

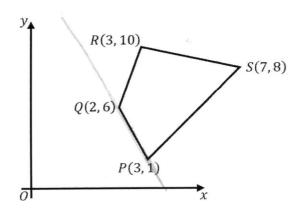

$R(3, 10)$

$S(7, 8)$

$Q(2, 6)$

$P(3, 1)$

**28**

$$f(x) = \frac{2x + 5}{3}$$

Sketch the graph of $f^{-1}(x)$ for $-2 \leq x \leq 3$

$y = \frac{2x + 5}{3}$

$2x$

$3y = 2x + 5$

$3y - 5 = 2x$

$\frac{3y - 5}{2} = x$

$\frac{3x - 5}{2} = y$

$\frac{-5}{2} = y$

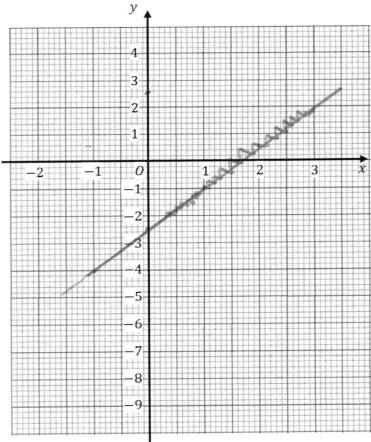

**29**

$f(x) = \cos x$

$g(x) = x - 90$

On the grid draw the graph of the function $fg(x)$ for $0° \leq x \leq 360°$

$f(g(x)) = \cos(x - 90)$

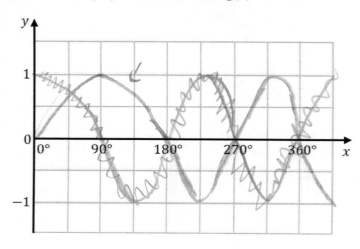

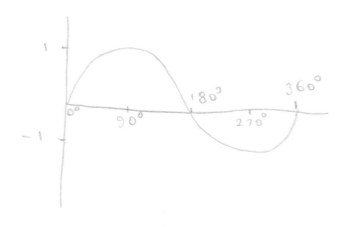

## Paper 2 Higher: Practice Set 1 Solutions

**1**

$$\frac{73}{1600} = 0.045625$$

The closest decimal is 0.04563 with a difference of 0.000005

**2**

Divide by 1000 to convert millimetres to metres.
This scale factor must be squared because there are 2 dimensions for areas:
$$48\text{mm}^2 \div 1000^2 = 0.000048\text{m}^2$$

**3**

A midpoint is the mean of the $x$ and $y$ coordinates:
$$\frac{3 + (-7)}{2} = -2 \qquad \text{and} \qquad \frac{8 + 16}{2} = 12$$
The midpoint of $A$ and $B$ is $(-2, 12)$

**4**

The difference between each term is $-6$ from e.g. $96 - 102 = -6$
This number is the coefficient of $n$: $-6n$
Subtract the difference from the first term in the sequence: $102 - (-6) = 108$
Add this value to the $-6n$ to give $-6n + 108$ or $108 - 6n$

**5**

There are 10 options if digits 0 to 9 are allowed.
The last digit is known to be prime, reducing the options to 4 numbers: 2, 3, 5 and 7.
One of these four will be correct, so the probability is $\frac{1}{4}$.

**6**

Use the product rule for counting by multiplying the number of options for each digit together.
The first digit is 4 (1 option).
The second digit can be any from 0 to 9 (10 options).
The third digit can be any from 0 to 9 (10 options).
The fourth digit must be odd (1, 3, 5, 7 or 9), so there are 5 options.
The product of all these options is $1 \times 10 \times 10 \times 5 = 500$
There are 500 possible codes.

**7(a)**

There are 6 calculations required to complete the table.
To avoid errors with the calculator, place brackets around the negative input values:
$$y = x^2 - 2x - 3$$
$$y = (-3)^2 - 2(-3) - 3$$
$$= 12$$
$$y = (-1)^2 - 2(-1) - 3$$
$$= 0$$
$$y = 1^2 - 2(1) - 3$$
$$= -4$$
$$y = 3^2 - 2(3) - 3$$
$$= 0$$
$$y = 5^2 - 2(5) - 3$$
$$= 12$$

| $x$ | $-3$ | $-1$ | 1 | 3 | 5 | 7 |
|---|---|---|---|---|---|---|
| $y$ | 12 | 0 | $-4$ | 0 | 12 | 32 |

$$y = 7^2 - 2(7) - 3$$
$$= 32$$

**7(b)**

Use the completed table below to plot the points:

| $x$ | $-3$ | $-1$ | 1 | 3 | 5 | 7 |
|---|---|---|---|---|---|---|
| $y$ | 12 | 0 | $-4$ | 0 | 12 | 32 |

The $y$-axis needs to go from at least $-4$ to 32
The $x$-axis needs to go from $-3$ to 7
A suggested correct graph is shown here.

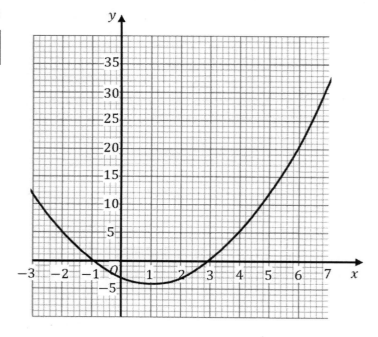

**7(c)**

The turning point of a quadratic graph can be found by completing the square:
$$y = x^2 - 2x - 3$$
$$= (x - 1)^2 - 1 - 3$$
$$= (x - 1)^2 - 4$$
For an equation of the form $y = (x + a)^2 + b$, the turning point is located at $(-a, b)$
The turning point of $y = (x - 1)^2 - 4$ is at $(1, -4)$

**8**

The right-angled triangle has opposite side $a$ and hypotenuse 9cm (with respect to the 55° angle).
Use **SOHCAHTOA** by selecting the sine function:

$$\sin 55° = \frac{\text{opposite}}{\text{hypotenuse}}$$
$$= \frac{a}{9}$$
$$9 \sin 55° = a$$
$$a = 7.37\text{cm (2dp)}$$

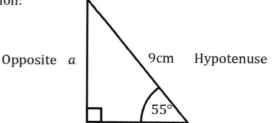

Opposite $a$    9cm    Hypotenuse

55°

**9(a)**

$$\text{average speed} = \frac{\text{total distance}}{\text{total time}}$$

The journey is split into 3 sections:
40 minutes is $\frac{2}{3}$ of an hour.
$$\text{distance} = \text{speed} \times \text{time}$$
$$= 60 \times \frac{2}{3}$$
$$= 40 \text{ miles}$$

The car stops for 15 minutes, bringing the journey time to 55 minutes.
The total journey time is 85 minutes, so the third part of the journey was completed in 30 minutes.
$\frac{30}{60} = \frac{1}{2}$ of an hour
distance = speed × time
$$= 56 \times \frac{1}{2}$$
$$= 28 \text{ miles}$$
The total journey distance:
$40 + 28 = 68$ miles
The total journey time in hours:
$\frac{85}{60} = \frac{17}{12}$ of an hour
The average speed for the journey:
$$\text{average speed} = \frac{\text{total distance}}{\text{total time}}$$
$$= \frac{68}{\frac{17}{12}}$$
$$= 48 \text{mph}$$

**9(b)**
20 minutes is $\frac{1}{3}$ of an hour, so the distance travelled at 60mph will be $60 \times \frac{1}{3} = 20$ miles
Draw a line from the origin to the point $(20,20)$
The car stopped for 10 minutes which is shown by a horizontal line (up to 30 minutes).
The journey was 90 minutes which means there are 60 minutes (or 1 hour) of travel time left.
The journey is completed at 50mph.
The distance travelled for this part will be 50 miles.
Draw a straight line from $(30, 20)$ up to $(90, 70)$

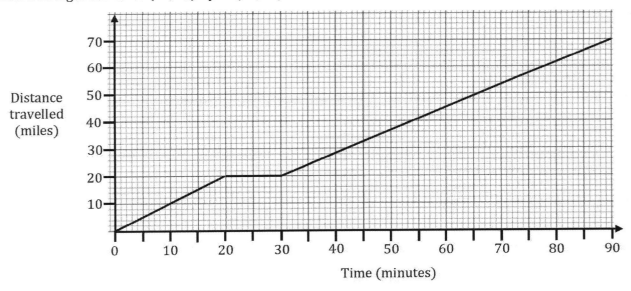

**10**
A probability is the same as a proportion.
If $\frac{1}{5}$ are terraced houses, 28 must be $\frac{1}{5}$ of all the houses.
$28 \times 5 = 140$
There are 140 houses in total.
Equate the sum of the expressions with 140 and solve for $x$:

$$2x + 9 + 4x + 28 + 13x + 8 = 140$$
$$19x + 45 = 140$$
$$19x = 95$$
$$x = 5$$

There are $13x + 8$ bungalows:

$$13(5) + 8 = 73$$

| Type of house | Detached | Semi-detached | Terraced | Bungalow |
|---|---|---|---|---|
| Number | 19 | 20 | 28 | 73 |

The probability of selecting a bungalow is $\frac{73}{140}$

## 11

1204 represents the difference between the number of fruit and the number of vegetables.
Find the difference in the angle size:

angle for vegetables $= 360° - 137°$
$$= 223°$$

difference in angle size $= 223° - 137°$
$$= 86°$$

This means that $86°$ represents 1204 objects in the pie chart.
Find how much $360°$ represents:

$$1204 \times \frac{360}{86} = 5040 \qquad \text{Divide by 86 for 1°, multiply by 360 for 360°}$$

There were 5040 fruit and vegetables altogether.

## 12

$4.75 \times 10^3 = 4750$
$4.7 \times 2^{10} = 4812.8$
$4.5 \times 3^6 = 3280.5$

The values in descending order (highest to lowest):
$4812.8, 4753, 4750, 3280.5$
The answer is:
$4.7 \times 2^{10}, \qquad 4753, \qquad 4.75 \times 10^3, \qquad 4.5 \times 3^6$

## 13

All 3 vertices lie on the circumference of the circle.
$BC$ will be a diameter if the angle opposite (angle $BAC$) is a right angle.

angle $BAC = 180° - 55° - 35°$
$$= 90°$$

Therefore, $BC$ is a diameter.

## 14

At least 109 cakes are required.
109 packets of flour and 654 eggs are needed to make 109 cakes.
The packets of flour come in multiples of 3 if the offer is used.
The nearest multiple of 3 to 109 is 108 ($36 \times 3$), with one extra packet required to make 109.
Each offer of flour costs $£1.20 \times 2 = £2.40$ (since you buy 2 and get a third free).
The offer will be used 36 times and one packet will be purchased individually:
$36 \times £2.40 + £1.20 = £87.60$
The eggs come in boxes of 15.
654 is not divisible by 15:
$$\frac{654}{15} = 43.6$$
44 boxes of eggs are required at £2.56 per box.
$44 \times £2.56 = £112.64$
The least total cost to make 109 cakes: $£87.60 + £112.64 = £200.24$

## 15

The graph is linear, so will have an equation of the form $y = mx + c$

The $y$-axis is $£C$ and the $x$-axis is $d$ days.

Find the gradient $m$ first:

Find two coordinate pairings from the graph, ideally ones with integer coordinates.

The two selected for this method are $(0, 140)$ and $(12, 740)$

$$m = \frac{740 - 140}{12 - 0}$$
$$= 50$$

Note that this means the digger costs £50 per day to hire.

$c$ is the $y$-intercept, which is at 140.

The equation of the formula:

$C = 50d + 140$

## 16(a)

The student has made an error in the expansion of $(x + 1)^2$ and $(x + 2)^2$

The student has squared the terms individually.

The working should read:

$$a^2 + b^2 = c^2$$
$$x^2 + (x + 1)^2 = (x + 2)^2$$
$$x^2 + x^2 + 2x + 1 = x^2 + 4x + 4$$
$$2x^2 + 2x + 1 = x^2 + 4x + 4$$
$$x^2 - 2x - 3 = 0$$
$$(x - 3)(x + 1) = 0$$

This means $x = 3$ or $x = -1$

Since $x$ is a positive side length, only $x = 3$ is a valid solution.

## 16(b)

Two triangles are similar if the ratio of the side lengths in each triangle is equal.

Solve for $x$ first using Pythagoras:

$$a^2 + b^2 = c^2$$
$$x^2 + (x + 1)^2 = (x + 2)^2$$
$$x^2 + x^2 + 2x + 1 = x^2 + 4x + 4$$
$$2x^2 + 2x + 1 = x^2 + 4x + 4$$
$$x^2 - 2x - 3 = 0$$
$$(x - 3)(x + 1) = 0$$

This means $x = 3$ or $x = -1$

$x = 3$ is the only valid solution, so the side lengths of the triangle are 3, 4 and 5.

This is a ratio of $3 : 4 : 5$

Solve for $y$ using Pythagoras:

$$a^2 + b^2 = c^2$$
$$y^2 + (y + 2)^2 = (y + 4)^2$$
$$y^2 + y^2 + 4y + 4 = y^2 + 8y + 16$$
$$2y^2 + 4y + 4 = y^2 + 8y + 16$$
$$y^2 - 4y - 12 = 0$$
$$(y - 6)(y + 2) = 0$$

This means $y = 6$ or $y = -2$

$y = 6$ is the only valid solution, so the side lengths of the triangle are 6, 8, 10

This simplifies to a ratio of $6 : 8 : 10 = 3 : 4 : 5$

The ratios are identical, so the triangles are similar.

**17**

The median value can be read directly from the box plot: it is the third vertical line which is 21.
The median is 21.

**18**

The length of $B$ is 30% more than $A$:
$80 \times 1.3 = 104$
The area of $A$ is $80a$ (rectangle: length × width).
The area of $B$ is $104b$ (parallelogram: length × perpendicular height).
The area of $B$ is 35% less than the area of $A$.
The multiplier for a 35% reduction is 0.65.
$104b = 0.65 \times 80a$
$104b = 52a$
$\quad 2b = a$
Using ratio, cross multiply the ratio $a : b = 2 : 1$

$2b = a$

$a : b$

$2 : 1$

**19(a)**

There are 4 missing entries in the Venn diagram.
Call them $a, b, c$ and $d$.
$\frac{1}{2}$ of the male members are members of the gym, so
$b = \dfrac{70}{2}$
$\quad = 35$
and $a = 35$
$\frac{1}{3}$ of the female members are members of the gym, so
$c = \dfrac{42}{3}$
$\quad = 14$
$d = 112 - 70 - 14$
$\quad = 28$

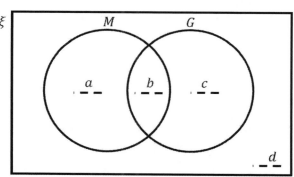

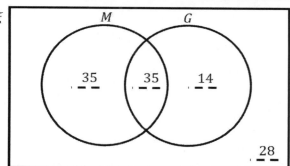

**19(b)**

"Given the member is male" means the denominator of the probability fraction will be the number of males:
$348 + 152 = 500$
The number of males who have been members for less than 10 years is 348.
The correct probability is $\frac{348}{500}$ or $\frac{87}{125}$ if simplified.

**20**

Divide the ratio to find the number of bags of each type of compost.
$4 + 9 + 12 = 25$
$325 \times \dfrac{4}{25} = 52$ small bags, $\qquad 325 \times \dfrac{9}{25} = 117$ medium bags, $\qquad 325 \times \dfrac{12}{25} = 156$ large bags
Let the volume of 1 small bag be $x$ litres.
The medium bag will be $2x$ litres and the large bag will be $5x$ litres.

Multiply each bag volume (in L litres) by the number of bags:

$52 \times x = 52x$ (L)small bags, $\qquad 117 \times 2x = 234x$ (L)medium bags, $\qquad 156 \times 5x = 780x$ (L)large bags

The total volume is 21320 litres:

$$52x + 234x + 780x = 21320$$
$$1066x = 21320$$
$$x = 20$$

One medium bag is $2x$ litres which is 40 litres.

## 21

There are side-angle opposite pairings in the triangle, so the sine rule can be used:

$$\frac{\sin x°}{7} = \frac{\sin 100°}{15}$$
$$\sin x° = \frac{7 \sin 100°}{15}$$
$$= 0.4595\ldots$$
$$x = \sin^{-1} 0.4595\ldots$$
$$= 27.4° \text{ (1dp)}$$

## 22

Solve this quadratic using the quadratic formula.

Get all the terms on the left-hand side of the equation:

$$4x^2 = 13x + 7$$
$$4x^2 - 13x - 7 = 0$$
$$a = 4, \qquad b = -13, \qquad c = -7$$
$$x = \frac{-b \pm \sqrt{b^2 - 4ac}}{2a}$$
$$= \frac{13 \pm \sqrt{(-13)^2 - 4(4)(-7)}}{2(4)}$$
$$x = 3.72, \qquad x = -0.470$$

## 23

Convert to a proportional statement:

$V \propto r^2$

Convert to an equation:

$V = kr^2$ where $k$ is the constant of proportionality.

Substitute $r = 5$ and $V = 150$ into the equation and solve for $k$:

$$150 = k \times 5^2$$
$$25k = 150$$
$$k = 6$$
$$V = 6r^2$$

Find the volume of a 7cm radius cylinder:

$$V = 6 \times 7^2$$
$$= 294$$

The increase in volume from a 5cm to 7cm cylinder is: $294 - 150 = 144\text{cm}^3$

## 24

$QRS$ will be a straight line if $\overrightarrow{QR}$ and $\overrightarrow{QS}$ are scalar multiples of each other.

$$\overrightarrow{QR} = \overrightarrow{QP} + \overrightarrow{PR}$$
$$= 2\mathbf{a} + 8\mathbf{b} + 2\mathbf{a} - 5\mathbf{b}$$
$$= 4\mathbf{a} + 3\mathbf{b}$$
$$\overrightarrow{QS} = \overrightarrow{QP} + \overrightarrow{PS}$$

$$= 2\mathbf{a} + 8\mathbf{b} + 6\mathbf{a} - 2\mathbf{b}$$
$$= 8\mathbf{a} + 6\mathbf{b}$$
$$= 2(4\mathbf{a} + 3\mathbf{b})$$
$$= 2\overrightarrow{QR}$$

Therefore $\overrightarrow{QR}$ and $\overrightarrow{QS}$ are scalar multiples of each other and $QRS$ is a straight line.

## 25

The interquartile range is the difference between the upper and lower quartiles.

The upper quartile will be where $\frac{3}{4}$ of the people is reached: $\frac{3}{4} \times 52 = 39$

The lower quartile will be where $\frac{1}{4}$ of the people is reached: $\frac{1}{4} \times 52 = 13$

Use the histogram to estimate where the 13th and 39th person will be.

The areas of the rectangles are equal to the frequencies.

The number of people from 0 to 10: $10 \times 0.8 = 8$

The number of people from 10 to 15: $5 \times 1.6 = 8$ (cumulative total is 16)

This means the 13th person is in the 10-15 age range.

Since the 0 to 10 age range had 8 people, we need a further 5 people to reach 13.

For the estimate assume that the 5th person (13th overall) in the 10 to 15 age range will be $\frac{5}{8}$ of the distance into the rectangle.

Multiply this proportion by the class width: $\frac{5}{8} \times 5 = 3.125$

Add this value to the age at the start of the class width: $10 + 3.125 = 13.125$

The lower quartile estimate is 13.125.

The number of people from 30 to 60: $30 \times 0.6 = 18$

This means the 39th person must be in the 30 to 60 age range.

For the estimate assume that the 39th person is $\frac{13}{18}$ of the distance back from 60.

Multiply this proportion by the class width: $\frac{13}{18} \times 30 = 21.7$

Subtract this value from 60: $60 - 21.7 = 38.3$

The upper quartile estimate is 38.3.

The interquartile range estimate:

$38.3 - 13.125 = 25.175$

Any answer from 25.1 to 25.3
would be acceptable as the estimate.

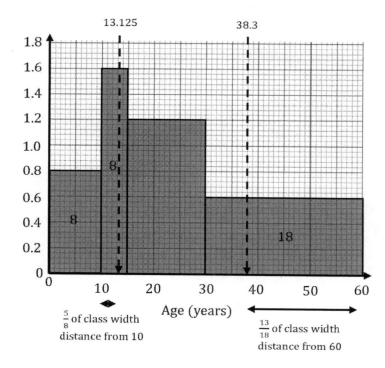

34

**26**

The sine area formula is used to find the area of the triangle.

The 3 semicircles are $\frac{3}{2}$ times the area of the circle (radius is 3cm).

$$\text{area of shape} = \frac{1}{2}ab\sin C + \frac{3}{2}\pi r^2$$
$$= \frac{1}{2} \times 6 \times 6 \times \sin 60° + \frac{3}{2} \times \pi \times 3^2$$
$$= 57.999\ldots$$

The area is $58.0\text{cm}^2$ (3sf).

**27(a)**

If a point remains invariant under an enlargement (where the scale factor is not 1) then the point must be the centre of the enlargement.

**27(b)**

If two points are invariant under a single transformation (with other points elsewhere), then the transformation is a reflection along a line that goes through the two points.

Find the equation of the line that goes through $P$ and $Q$:

$$y = mx + c$$
$$m = \frac{6-1}{2-3}$$
$$= -5$$
$$y = -5x + c$$

Substitute the point $(3, 1)$ into the equation to find $c$:

$$1 = -5(3) + c$$
$$1 = -15 + c$$
$$c = 16$$

The transformation is a reflection in the line $y = -5x + 16$

**28**

Let the function $f(x) =$ be replaced with $y =$

$$y = \frac{2x+5}{3}$$

Find the inverse function first by swapping $y$ for $x$ and $x$ for $y$.

Then make the new $y$ the subject:

$$x = \frac{2y+5}{3}$$
$$3x = 2y + 5$$
$$3x - 5 = 2y$$
$$y = \frac{3x-5}{2}, \qquad \text{so } f^{-1}(x) = \frac{3x-5}{2}$$

This function can be rewritten as $f^{-1}(x) = \frac{3}{2}x - \frac{5}{2}$

This is a straight line with gradient $\frac{3}{2}$ and $y$-intercept $-\frac{5}{2}$

Two through points are needed for a straight line.

Use $x = -2$ and $x = 3$ to find the points:

$$f^{-1}(-2) = \frac{3(-2)-5}{2}$$
$$= -\frac{11}{2}$$
$$f^{-1}(3) = \frac{3(3)-5}{2}$$
$$= 2$$

Plot the two points $\left(-2, -\frac{11}{2}\right)$ and $(3, 2)$

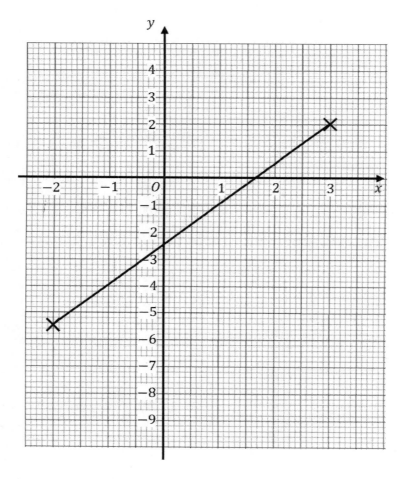

**29**

$$fg(x) = f(x - 90)$$
$$= \cos(x - 90)$$

This is a translation of $\begin{pmatrix} 90 \\ 0 \end{pmatrix}$

The graph of $y = \cos x$ is moved 90° to the right as shown below.

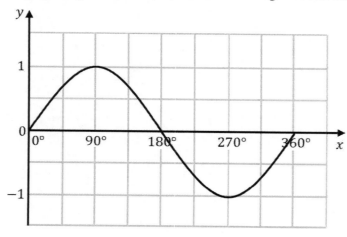

## Paper 3 Higher: Practice Set 1

**1**

$\mathbf{a} = \begin{pmatrix} 2 \\ -5 \end{pmatrix}$ and $\mathbf{b} = \begin{pmatrix} -3 \\ 7 \end{pmatrix}$

Circle the vector $3\mathbf{a} - \mathbf{b}$

$\begin{pmatrix} 3 \\ -17 \end{pmatrix}$ $\qquad$ $\begin{pmatrix} 9 \\ -17 \end{pmatrix}$ $\qquad$ $\begin{pmatrix} 3 \\ -3 \end{pmatrix}$ $\qquad$ $\begin{pmatrix} 9 \\ -22 \end{pmatrix}$

**2**

What value of $x$ would make $1.25 \times 10^x$ a cube number?
Circle your answer.

0 $\qquad$ 1 $\qquad$ 2 $\qquad$ 3

**3**

Rearrange $3p = \frac{2q}{r}$ to make $r$ the subject.

$r = \frac{3p}{2q}$ $\qquad$ $r = \frac{2q}{3p}$ $\qquad$ $r = \frac{3q}{2p}$ $\qquad$ $r = \frac{2p}{3q}$

**4**

What is the bearing of $A$ from $B$?
Circle your answer.

$180 - 48$

$= 132$

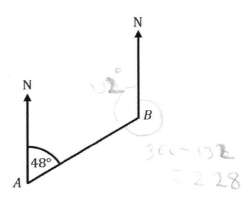

$360 - 132$

$= 228$

228° $\qquad$ 132° $\qquad$ 312° $\qquad$ 42°

**5**

A six-sided dice lands on five 300 times.
The relative frequency of five is 0.2.
How many times was the dice rolled?

$15 \times 0.1$

$= 1500$ times

**6**

Find the integer solutions that satisfy the following inequalities:

$11 < 4x + 3 \le 31$ $\qquad$ $8 < 4x \le 28$ $\qquad$ $2 < x \le 7$ $\qquad$ 3, 4, 5, 6, 7

$-6 \le 4x \le 16$ $\qquad$ $-6 \le 4x \le 16$ $\qquad$ $-1.5 \le x \le 4$ $\qquad$ -1, 0, 1, 2, 3, 4

**7**

The length of a log is 23m to the nearest metre.
Complete the error interval for the length $l$ of the log.

$22.5 \le x < 23.5$

**8**

$210 \le x < 220$ =. $21cm \le x < 22cm$

The length of a brick is 215mm correct to the nearest 5mm.
11 of these bricks are joined together in a line.

$21 \times 11 = 231$          $22 \times 11 = 242$

A bricklayer says the combined length is 239cm correct to the nearest centimetre.
Show that this could be correct.

$231cm \le x < 242$

**9**

A shape is formed from two triangles and two congruent sectors.
If the triangles are equilateral, find the angle $x$.

$360 = 2x + 120$

$240 = 2x$

$120° = x$

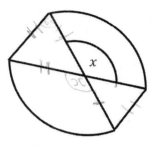

**10**

There are 840 B roads and 600 A roads in a country.

The probability that a B road, chosen at random, has roadworks on it is $\frac{3}{10}$.

$\frac{252}{840}$          $252 + 125 = 377$

$840 + 600 = 1440$

The probability that an A road, chosen at random, has roadworks on it is $\frac{5}{24}$. $= \frac{125}{600}$

$1440 - 377$

Work out how many roads do not have roadworks.

$1063$

**11**

$AB, CD$ and $EF$ are straight lines.

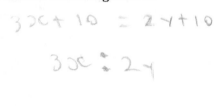

$3x + 10 = 2y + 10$

$3x = 2y$

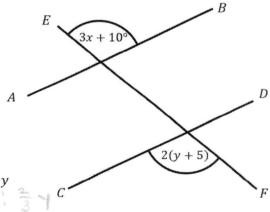

If $AB$ and $CD$ are parallel, find the ratio $x : y$

$x : \frac{2}{3}y$

**12**

$AB, CD$ and $EF$ are straight lines.

$360 = 8x + 20 + (100 - 2y)$

$= 120 - 8x - 2y$

$240 = 8x - 2y$

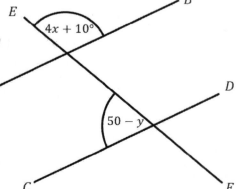

$AB$ and $CD$ are parallel.
If $x$ increased by 5°, what happens to the value of $y$?
$(4x + 10)$ is obtuse and $(50 - y)$ is acute.

**13**

Orange squash is made from orange concentrate and water mixed in the ratio 2 : 7
There are 250ml of orange concentrate and 840ml of water available.
What is the maximum amount of orange squash that can be made?

$\frac{840}{7} = 120$

$120 \times 2 = 240 ml$

**14**

$(xt^y)^5 \equiv 32t^{15}$ where $x$ and $y$ are integers.
Work out $x$ and $y$.    $x = 2$    $2^5 = 32$    $Y = 3$    $3 \times 5 = 15$

**15**

A box is full of 32 items of fruit.
There are 12 apples and the rest are pears.
The mean weight of the apples is 205g.
The mean weight of all the fruit is 200.625g.
Work out the mean weight of the pears.

$200.625 \times 32 = 6420g$

$205 \times 12 = 2460$

$6420 - 2460 = 3960g$    $32 - 12 = 20$

$3960 / 20 = 198$

**16**

$xy = k$
$k$ is a constant.
If $x$ doubles, what happens to $y$?    $Y/2$

**17**

$F = \dfrac{k}{r^2}$
$k$ is a constant.
How is $F$ proportionally related to $r$?    Inversely porportional

**18**

The graph shows the distance of a planet from a star as it orbits over a period of 70 days.

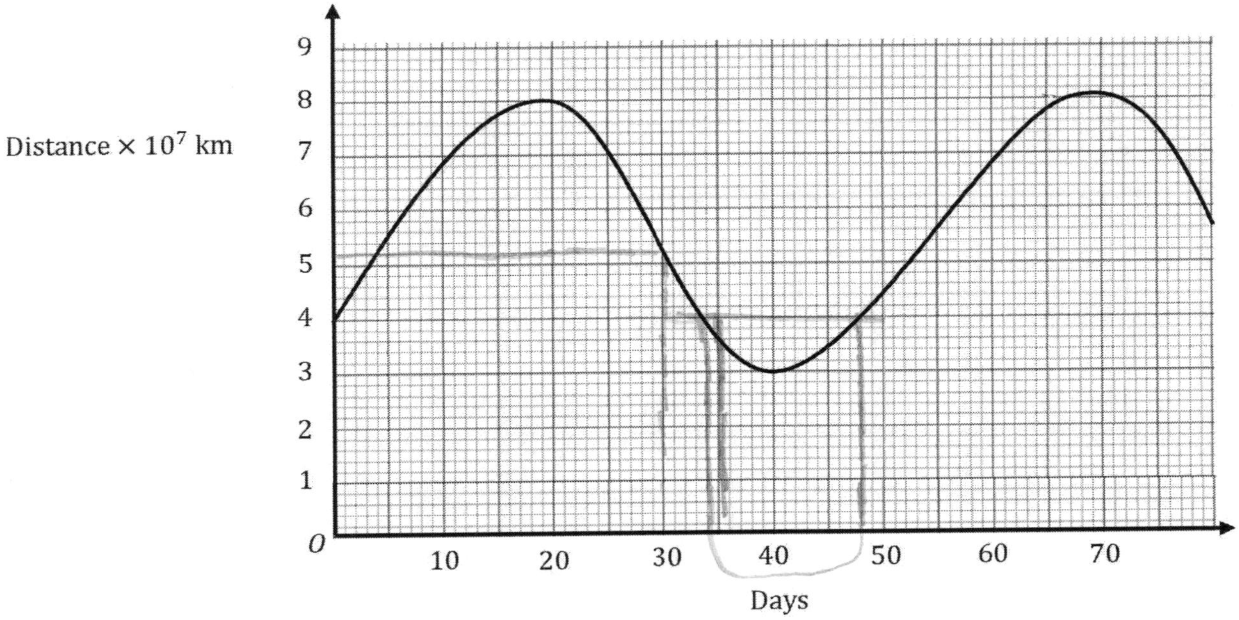

Distance $\times 10^7$ km

Days

**(a)**

How far is the planet from the star at 30 days?    $5.1 \times 10^7 km$

**(b)**

When the planet is within 40 million km of the star the surface temperatures reach over 1600°C.
Estimate how many days the surface temperature is over 1600°C.    14

$48 - 34 = 14$

**19**

The value of an investment is initially £12000.

The value of the investment decreases by 20% in each of the first two years.

The value of the investment increases by 15% in each of the next three years.

How much is the investment worth at the end of the five years?

*[handwritten: $12000 \times 0.8 = 9600$]*

*[handwritten: $9600 \times 0.8 = 7680$]*

*[handwritten: $768 \times 1.15^3$]*

*[handwritten: £11680.32]*

**20**

A hybrid car is driven.

The car travels 12 miles in 15 minutes. *[handwritten: 48mph]*

The car then travels at 60mph for 1 hour 24 minutes. *[handwritten: 84 miles]*

The manufacturers claim the following:

If the average speed is less than 50mph, the car will do 80 miles per gallon.

If the average speed is 50mph or above, the car will do 56 miles per gallon.

Find the amount of fuel used by the car.

**21**

What is wrong with the following sketch graph? *[handwritten: starts at 1]*

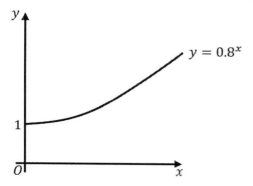

**22**

$A, B, C$ and $D$ are points on a circle.

$AEC$ and $BED$ are straight lines.

$AB = AE = ED$

Find the value of $x$.

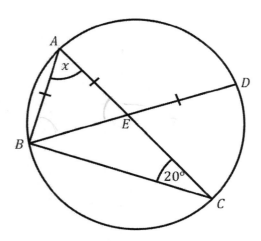

**23**

A pedestrian bridge has a safety sign:

Total weight of people on bridge must not exceed 2000kg.

There are 24 people on the bridge with a mean weight of 80kg given to the nearest 5kg.

Another person gets onto the bridge.

Their weight is 90kg to the nearest kg.

Will the safety limit be exceeded?

*[handwritten: 80 ~~k~~   $75 \leq x \leq 85$]*

*[handwritten: 85 ≤]*

*[handwritten: $89.5 \leq x < 90.5$]*

**24**

The sketch of the quadratic function f($x$) is shown below.
The graph intersects the $x$-axis at $x = -6.6$ and $x = 3.4$
Write down the interval defined by f($x$) $\leq 0$

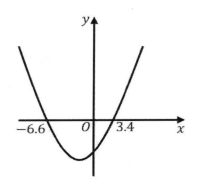

**25**

Work out an expression for the $n$th term of the quadratic sequence:

3        7        15        27        ...

$t_n = 2n^2 - 2n + 3$

**26**

The curve shows a sketch of $y = x^2 + ax + b$
The curve intersects the $x$-axis at $(6, 0)$ and at point $M$.
The curve intersects the $y$-axis at $(0, -12)$
Find the coordinates of the turning point of the graph.

correction

$b = -12$

$0 = 6^2 + 6a - 12$
$36 + 6a$
$24 + 6a$
$a = -4$

$y = x^2 - 4x$
$(x-2)^2 - 2^2 - 12 = (x-2)^2 - 16$

$x = 2$
$y = -16$

$(2, -16)$

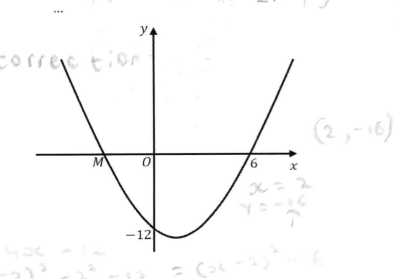

**27**

A tennis ball is thrown from the top of a building 5m above the ground.
Estimate the speed of the tennis ball 2 seconds after it is thrown in m/s.

2.05 m/s

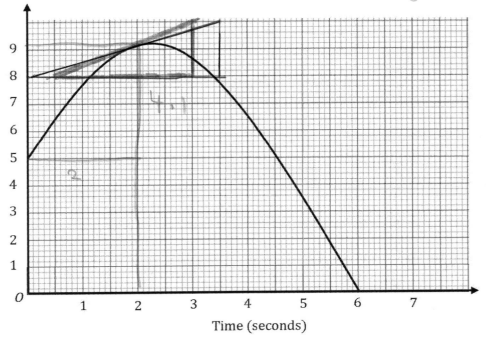

line
to
motion

²/2.5

Point

41

is the correction        $\frac{2}{3.5} = 0.57$ m/s

**28**

A triangular prism is shown below.
$AD = 50$cm    $EC = 8$cm
The volume of the prism is 6000cm³.
Find the angle $EAB$.

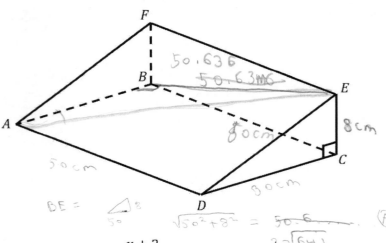

$\frac{1}{2} \cancel{B}^{W} \times H \times L$

$\frac{1}{2} \times 50 \times 8 \times W = 6000$

$W = \cancel{\frac{6000}{}} 30$cm .

$\tan^{-1}\left(\frac{2\sqrt{641}}{30}\right)$

$= 59.4°$

$BE = \underset{50}{\triangle}^{8}$

$\sqrt{50^2 + 8^2} = 50.6$

$2\sqrt{641}$     (A)

**29**

The shape shown has rotational symmetry 2.
All measurements are in centimetres.
The area of the shape is 180cm².
Find the value of $x$.

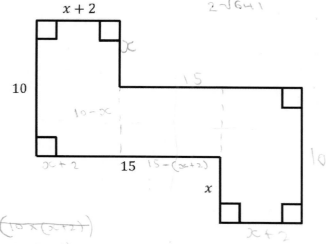

$(\overset{x+10}{\cancel{10+x}})(x+17)$

$x^2 + 27x + 170 = 180$

$x^2 + 27x \le 10$

$2(10 \times (x+2))$

$2 \times 10 \times (x+2)$

$20(x+2) + (10-x)[15-(x+2)]$

$20x + 40 + 150 - 10x\bar{+}20 - 15x + x^2 \bar{+} 2x$

$20x - 10x - 15x \bar{+} 2x + x^2 + 40 + 150 \cancel{+} 20$

$x^2 \cancel{-7x + 200}$

$x^2 - 3x + 170 = 180$

$x^2 - 3x \cancel{+} 10 \ge 0$

$(x-5)(x+2)$

$x = 5 \text{ or } -2$

$x = 5$

**30**

Prove that $6x - x^2 - 15$ is always negative.

$-x^2 + 6x - 15$

$-[x^2 - 6x + 15]$

$\cancel{\underset{}{}} - [(x-3)^2 - 9 + 15]$

$-[(x-3)^2 + 6]$

$-(x-3)^2 \le 0$     $-(x-3)^2 - 6$

$-(x-3)^2 - 6 \le -6$     $< 0$

42

**1**

$$3\mathbf{a} - \mathbf{b} = 3\begin{pmatrix} 2 \\ -5 \end{pmatrix} - \begin{pmatrix} -3 \\ 7 \end{pmatrix}$$
$$= \begin{pmatrix} 6 \\ -15 \end{pmatrix} - \begin{pmatrix} -3 \\ 7 \end{pmatrix}$$
$$= \begin{pmatrix} 9 \\ -22 \end{pmatrix}$$

**2**

The cube number with the digits 1, 2 and 5 is 125.
$1.25 \times 10^2 = 125$
$x = 2$

**3**

$$3p = \frac{2q}{r}$$
$$3pr = 2q$$
$$r = \frac{2q}{3p}$$

**4**

Bearings are measured from north in a clockwise direction.
Start at the north at $B$.
The north directions are parallel.
Using corresponding angles, the bearing is the sum of $48° + 180° = 228°$
The bearing of $A$ from $B$ is $228°$

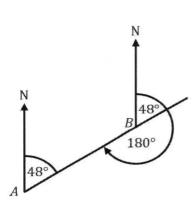

**5**

The relative frequency is the same as a probability (which means it is a proportion).
$0.2 = \frac{1}{5}$ which means that $\frac{1}{5}$ of the dice rolls is 300.
$300 \times 5 = 1500$
The dice was rolled 1500 times.

**6**

Solve the inequalities first:
$11 < 4x + 3 \le 31$
$8 < 4x \le 28$
$2 < x \le 7$
This represents the integers 3, 4, 5, 6 and 7.
$-6 \le 4x \le 16$
$-1.5 \le x \le 4$
This represents the integers $-1, 0, 1, 2, 3$ and 4.
The integer solutions that satisfy both inequalities are 3 and 4.

**7**

The log is measured in metre units.
The nearest metre is the same as the nearest whole number.
This is the units place value (1's).

Divide this place value by 2:
$$\frac{1}{2} = 0.5$$
This means the length is measured to $23 \pm 0.5$m
The error interval for the length of the log is $22.5 \le l < 23.5$

## 8

If the error interval of 11 bricks and the error interval of the combined lengths overlap, the statement of the bricklayer is correct.
The bricks are measured in millimetres and rounded to the nearest 5mm.
Divide this value by 2:
$$\frac{5}{2} = 2.5$$
This means the brick lengths (call this $l$) are measured to $215 \pm 2.5$mm
The error interval of a single brick (in mm) is $212.5 \le l < 217.5$
The error interval of 11 bricks (in mm) is $2337.5 \le l < 2392.5$  [1]
The bricklayer measured the length of 11 bricks in centimetres to the nearest cm (units column).
Divide this value by 2:
$$\frac{1}{2} = 0.5$$
This means the length of 11 bricks (call this $x$) is $239 \pm 0.5$cm
The error interval for the measured length (in cm) is $238.5 \le x < 239.5$
Convert this error interval into mm to compare error intervals: $2385 \le x < 2395$  [2]
The intervals overlap for the values 2385 up to 2392.5.
Hence the bricklayer could be correct.

## 9

The sectors are congruent, so the other sector has angle $x$.
The triangles are equilateral, so each interior angle is 60°.
$x$ can be found by considering angles at a point sum to 360°:
$$x = \frac{360 - 120}{2}$$
$$= 120°$$

## 10

Use the probabilities as proportional multipliers to find the number of roads without roadworks.
$1 - \frac{3}{10} = \frac{7}{10}$, so $\frac{7}{10}$ of B roads do not have roadworks.
$\frac{7}{10} \times 840 = 588$, so 588 B roads do not have roadworks.
$1 - \frac{5}{24} = \frac{19}{24}$, so $\frac{19}{24}$ of A roads do not have roadworks.
$\frac{19}{24} \times 600 = 475$, so 475 A roads do not have roadworks.
$588 + 475 = 1063$ roads that do not have roadworks.

## 11

If $AB$ and $CD$ are parallel, the two given angles are equal:
Opposite angles are equal and alternate angles are equal.
$3x + 10 = 2(y + 5)$
$3x + 10 = 2y + 10$
$\qquad 3x = 2y$
Using ratio, cross multiply: $x : y = 2 : 3$

$3x = 2y$

$x : y$

$2 : 3$

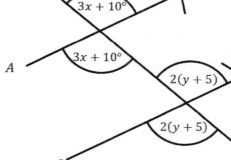

**12**

If $AB$ and $CD$ are parallel, the two given angles sum to $180°$ (by corresponding and allied angles).
To understand what happens to $y$ as $x$ increases by $5°$, an equation with $y$ as the subject is required.
$50 - y + 4x + 10 = 180$
$$4x - y = 120$$
$y = 4x - 120$
If $x$ increases by $5°$, the value of $y$ will increase by $20°$, e.g. when $x = 35, y = 20$ and when $x = 40, y = 40$

**13**

The maximum volume of orange squash will be made when the first limiting ingredient runs out.
If 250ml of orange concentrate are used, then 2 parts is 250ml.
This means 1 part is 125ml.
The amount of water required is $7 \times 125 = 875$ml
This is not possible since only 840ml of water are available.
Water is the limiting ingredient.
If 840ml of water are used, then 7 parts is 840ml.
This means that 1 part is 120ml.
The amount of orange concentrate required is $2 \times 120 = 240$ml
Adding these two volumes: $840 + 240 = 1080$ml
The maximum volume of orange squash that can be made is 1080ml.

**14**

The symbol $\equiv$ is an identity.
Both sides are identical to each other.
Use the law of indices on the left-hand side:
$(xt^y)^5 = x^5 t^{5y}$
$x^5 t^{5y} \equiv 32t^{15}$
Two equations can be formed: the first from the coefficient of $t^{5y}$ and the second from the indices.
$x^5 = 32$
$x = 2$
$5y = 15$
$y = 3$

**15**

The known data can be summarised in a table (shown in bold):

|  | Frequency | Mean | Frequency × Mean |
|---|---|---|---|
| Apples | **12** | **205** | $12 \times 205 = 2460$ |
| Pears | 20 | 198 | 3960 |
| All fruit | **32** | **200.625** | $32 \times 200.625 = 6420$ |

Number of pears: $32 - 12 = 20$
Total weight of apples: $12 \times 205 = 2460$
Total weight of all fruit: $32 \times 200.625 = 6420$
Total weight of pears: $6420 - 2460 = 3960$

Mean weight of pears: $\frac{3960}{20} = 198$
The correct answer is 198g.

**16**

$xy = k$ can be rearranged to make $y$ the subject:

$$y = \frac{k}{x}$$

This equation is of the form "$y$ is inversely proportional to $x$".
This means that $y$ will change in exactly the opposite proportional way to $x$.
If $x$ doubles then $y$ will halve.

**17**

$$F = \frac{k}{r^2}$$

$r$ is in the denominator which means it is an inverse proportion.
$F$ is inversely proportional to the square of $r$.
Also acceptable:
$F$ is directly proportional to $\frac{1}{r^2}$

**18(a)**
Draw a line upwards from 30 days to the curve.
Answers between $5.2 \times 10^7$ and $5.4 \times 10^7$ km are acceptable.

**18(b)**
Draw a line across from $4 \times 10^7$ km (40 million km) to the curve.
The line intersects the curve at approximately 34 days and 48 days.
The time interval between these days is when the planet is within 40 million km.
$48 - 34 = 14$
The answer is close to 14 days.

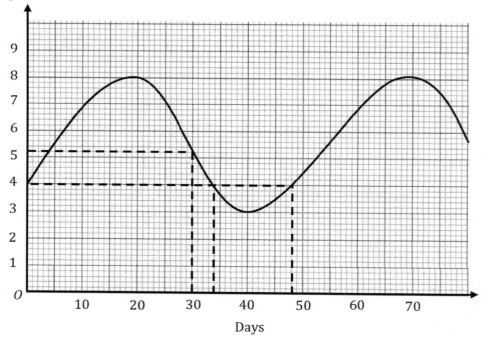

Distance $\times 10^7$ km

Days

**19**
The multiplier to decrease by 20% is 0.8
The multiplier to increase by 15% is 1.15
Raise each multiplier to the power of the number of years it is applied:
£12000 $\times 0.8^2 \times 1.15^3 = $ £11680.32
The investment is worth £11680.32 at the end of five years.

**20**

There are two stages to the overall journey.
The fuel economy is dictated by the average speed.
Find the speed of the car for the first part of the journey:
Convert 15 minutes into hours: $\frac{15}{60} = \frac{1}{4}$ of an hour

$$\text{speed} = \frac{\text{distance}}{\text{time}}$$
$$= \frac{12}{\frac{1}{4}}$$
$$= 48\text{mph}$$

At 48mph, the car is travelling 80 miles per gallon of fuel.
The car travels 12 miles, so the car uses $\frac{12}{80} = \frac{3}{20}$ gallons
The car travels at 60mph for the second part of the journey and so uses 56 miles per gallon.
Find the distance travelled to calculate the fuel consumption:
Convert 1 hour 24 minutes into hours: $\frac{84}{60} = 1.4$ hours

$$\text{distance} = \text{speed} \times \text{time}$$
$$= 60 \times 1.4$$
$$= 84\text{miles}$$

The car travels 84 miles, so the car used $\frac{84}{56} = \frac{3}{2}$ gallons

The total amount of fuel used by the car is $\frac{3}{20} + \frac{3}{2} = \frac{33}{20}$ gallons

This can be given as 1.65 gallons.

**21**

This is an exponential graph with a base (0.8) that is between 0 and 1.
This means the shape of the graph will be a decreasing function as shown:

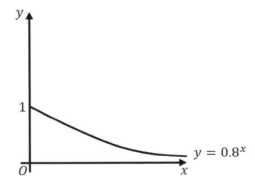

**22**

Join the points $AD$.
Angle $ADB$ is equal to angle $BCA$.
(They are both 20° because they are angles in the same segment.)
$AE = ED$, so triangle $AED$ is isosceles.
Angle $EAD$ is also 20° because triangle $AED$ is isosceles.
Angle $BEC$ is 140°.
Angle $AEB$ is 40° (180° on a straight line).
$x = 100°$ since triangle $ABE$ is isosceles.

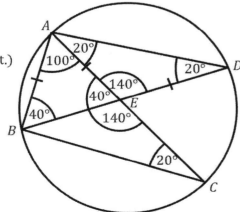

47

**23**

Find the error interval for the mass of people on the bridge.

The mean weight of the 24 people is 80kg to the nearest 5kg.

Halve this value: $\frac{5}{2} = 2.5$ which means the mean weight is $80 \pm 2.5$kg.

The error interval for the mean weight is $77.5 \leq$ mean weight of $24 < 82.5$

Multiply this error interval by 24 to get the total weight of the 24 people on the bridge:

$77.5 \times 24 = 1860$kg and $82.5 \times 24 = 1980$kg: $1860 \leq$ weight of $24 < 1980$

The error interval for the extra person is $89.5 \leq$ weight $< 90.5$

The error interval for all 25 people is formed by adding the error intervals:

$1860 + 89.5 \leq$ weight of $25 < 1980 + 90.5$

$1949.5 \leq$ weight of $25 < 2070.5$

This error interval overlaps the safety limit of 2000kg.

The correct conclusion is "the safety limit may be exceeded".

**24**

$f(x) \leq 0$ is the region of the graph below the $x$-axis.

This is given by the interval $-6.6 \leq x \leq 3.4$

**25**

Find the second difference:

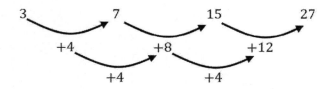

The second difference is 4.

Halve the second difference: $\frac{4}{2} = 2$

This number is the coefficient of $n^2$: $2n^2$

Write out the sequence of $2n^2$:

| 2 | 8 | 18 | 32 | ... |

Subtract this sequence from the original sequence:

| 1 | $-1$ | $-3$ | $-5$ | ... |

This sequence is a linear sequence which has $n$th term $-2n + 3$

Add this linear sequence $n$th term to the $2n^2$ from earlier: $2n^2 - 2n + 3$

The correct expression is $2n^2 - 2n + 3$

**26**

Substitute the coordinates into the equation to find the unknown values $a$ and $b$.

For $(6, 0)$:

$0 = 6^2 + 6a + b$

$0 = 36 + 6a + b$ [1]

For $(0, -12)$:

$-12 = 0^2 + 0 + b$

$b = -12$

Substitute this into equation [1]:

$0 = 36 + 6a - 12$
$6a = -24$
$a = -4$
The equation is $y = x^2 - 4x - 12$
Complete the square to find the turning point:
$y = (x - 2)^2 - 4 - 12$
$y = (x - 2)^2 - 16$
The turning point of the quadratic with equation $y = (x + a)^2 + b$ has coordinates $(-a, b)$
The turning point has coordinates $(2, -16)$

**27**
The gradient on a distance-time graph gives the speed.
Use a ruler to approximate the gradient at the point on the curve when the time is 2 seconds.
Draw a tangent at time = 2 seconds.
Form a right-angled triangle from the tangent line and calculate the gradient:
$$\text{gradient} = \frac{1.8}{3.7}$$
$$= 0.49$$
The speed is approximately 0.49m/s; answers of $0.49 \pm 0.02$m/s are acceptable.

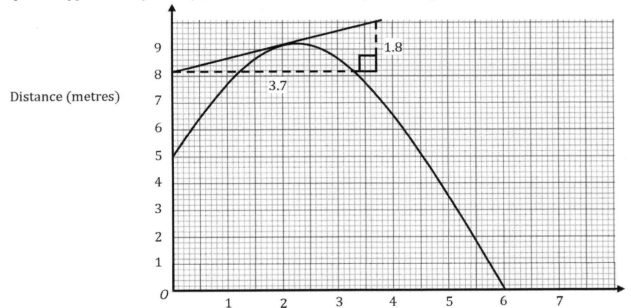

Distance (metres)

Time (seconds)

**28**
Angle $EAB$ is part of the triangle $EAB$.
This triangle has a right-angle at $ABE$.
Two side lengths are required to find another angle in triangle $EAB$ (the sides are $BE$ and $AB$).
$AD = BC$ since the shape is a prism.
$BC$ is 50cm and $EC$ is 8cm.
Triangle $BEC$ is right-angled.
Use Pythagoras to find the length $BE$:
$$a^2 + b^2 = c^2$$
$$BC^2 + EC^2 = BE^2$$
$$50^2 + 8^2 = BE^2$$

$$2564 = BE^2$$
$$BE = \sqrt{2564}$$

Use the prism volume formula to find the length of $AB$:

volume = cross sectional area × length

$$6000 = \frac{1}{2} \times AB \times BF \times AD$$

$$6000 = \frac{1}{2} \times AB \times 8 \times 50$$

$$= 200 \times AB$$

$$AB = 30$$

Use SOHCAH**TOA** on triangle $EAB$:

$$\tan(\text{angle } EAB) = \frac{\text{opposite}}{\text{adjacent}}$$

$$= \frac{\sqrt{2564}}{30}$$

$$= 1.687 \dots$$

$$\text{angle } EAB = \tan^{-1} \frac{\sqrt{2564}}{30}$$

$$= 59.4° \ (1dp)$$

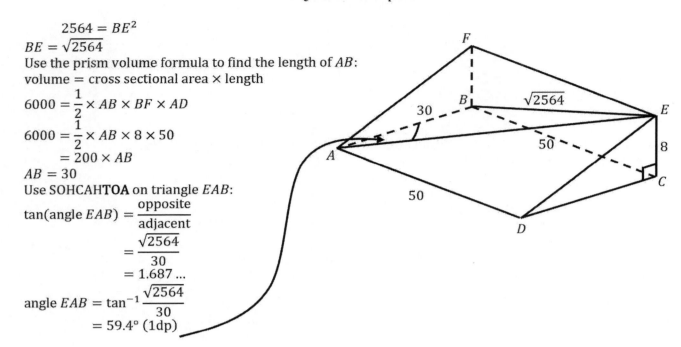

**29**

The shape has rotational symmetry 2, so the unlabelled side lengths are all known.

The shape can be thought of as a large rectangle with two smaller rectangles removed from 2 corners.

The expression for the area of the shape is equal to 180.

$$(10 + x)(15 + x + 2) - 2 \times 15x = 180$$
$$(10 + x)(17 + x) - 30x = 180$$
$$170 + 27x + x^2 - 30x = 180$$
$$x^2 - 3x + 170 = 180$$
$$x^2 - 3x - 10 = 0$$
$$(x - 5)(x + 2) = 0$$

$x = 5$ or $x = -2$

Since $x$ is a length only $x = 5$ is valid.

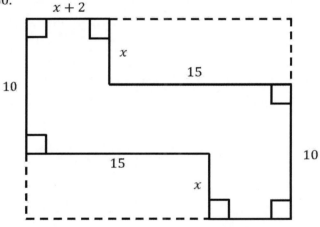

**30**

Rearrange the expression so that the $x^2$ term is first.

Factor out the $-1$ from the $-x^2$ and $6x$ terms.

Complete the square and simplify.

The correct proof is shown below:

$$6x - x^2 - 15 = -x^2 + 6x - 15$$
$$= -(x^2 - 6x) - 15$$
$$= -((x - 3)^2 - 9) - 15$$
$$= -(x - 3)^2 + 9 - 15$$
$$= -(x - 3)^2 - 6$$

$(x - 3)^2$ is greater than or equal to zero.

$-(x - 3)^2$ is less than or equal to zero.

$-(x - 3)^2 - 6$ is less than zero for all values of $x$.

Therefore, $6x - x^2 - 15$ is always negative.

## Paper 1 Higher: Practice Set 2

**1**

Work out $\sqrt{3^4 + 12^2}$  $\sqrt{81 + 144} = \sqrt{225}$

Circle your answer.

11̷2.5          2̷25          21          (15)

**2**

What is three billion in standard form?

Circle your answer.

$3 \times 10^{12}$          $300 \times 10^8$          (($3 \times 10^9$))          $0.3 \times 10^{10}$   ✓

**3**

Circle the expression equivalent to $(3c^5)^4$

$3c^{20}$          $12c^{20}$          ($81c^{20}$)          $12c^9$   ✓

**4**

$R = \dfrac{20}{A}$

If $A$ is increased by 100%, by what percentage does $R$ change?

Circle your answer.

100%          (50%)          20%          5%   ✓

**5**   ✓

Factorise $y^2 - 121$          $(y + 11)(y - 11)$

**6**

Solve $9x + 7 \geq 5 + 4x$          $5x \geq -2$          ✓
$x \geq -\frac{2}{5}$

**7**

Work out the value of $\left(\sqrt{27}\right)^3 \times \left(\sqrt{3}\right)^3$
$27\sqrt{27} \times 3\sqrt{3} = 81\sqrt{81} = 81 \times 9$
$= 8^0 \, 729$   ✓

**8**

A sector has radius 9cm.

Find the area of the sector in terms of $\pi$.
$\pi r^2 \times \frac{120}{360}$

$81\pi \times \frac{1}{3} = 27\pi \ cm^2$   ✓

120°

**9**

Five whole numbers are rounded to the nearest 100.
The mean of the rounded numbers is 80.
Find the maximum possible sum of the original five numbers.
~~645~~ 645   ✓

$0 + (100 \times 4) = 400/5 = 80$

$49 + (149 \times 4) =$

$449 + (49 \times 4) = 449 + (200 - 4) =$

$649 - 4 = 645$

**10**

$n$ is an integer.
The next 4 consecutive integers are added to $n$.
Find the mean of the 5 consecutive integers in terms of $n$.

$n + (n+1) + (n+2) + (n+3) + (n+4)$

$5n + 10$

 $n + 2$   ✓

51

**11**

A parallelogram is formed from four identical isosceles trapeziums.
Each trapezium has height $h$.
The parallel sides of the trapezium have lengths $a$ and $2a$.

**(a)**

Find an expression for the area of the parallelogram in terms of $a$ and $h$.

$h(2a-a) = ah \qquad 3a \times 2h = 6ah$

**(b)**

$a : h = 2 : 3$

Find an expression in terms of $a$ for the perimeter of the parallelogram.

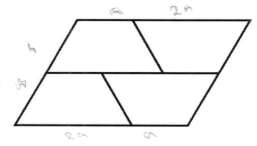

**12**

Four types of bird were observed in a garden.
The pie chart shows the proportion of each type of bird in the garden.
Work out the probability that a bird observed is a house sparrow.

$360 - 70 = 290°$

$290° = 6x - 10$

$\dfrac{300°}{360} = 6x$

$50° = x$

$100° = 2x$

$\dfrac{100}{360} = \dfrac{10}{36} = \dfrac{5}{18}$

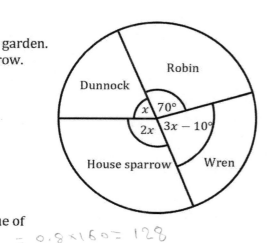

**13**

Use approximations to 1 significant figure to estimate the value of

$$\dfrac{0.848 \times 37.4^2}{\sqrt{109.34}}$$

$\dfrac{0.8 \times 40^2}{\sqrt{100}} = \dfrac{0.8 \times 1600}{10} = 0.8 \times 160 = 128$

**14**

$a : b = 3 : 11 \qquad 14$

$3(a + b) = 462$

Find the value of $3(a - b)$

$99 \quad 363$

$3a + 3b = 462$

$99 - 363 = 726 \quad 396$

$99 - 363 = -264$

$14\overline{)462} \quad ^{0\,3\,3}$

$3 \times 33 = 99$

$3 \times 11 = 363$

**15**

Two congruent decagons are joined together.
Find the size of the angle $x$.

$360 / 10 = 36$

$36 \times 2 = x$

$72° = x \quad \checkmark$

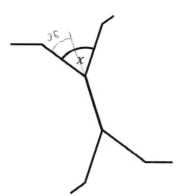

**16**

A plant nursery is offering a deal on packets of seed: choose one vegetable, one fruit and one herb.
There are 25 different vegetables, 12 different fruits and 8 different herbs.
How many different combinations are there?

$25 \times 12 \times 8 =$

$300 \times 8 = 2400 \quad \checkmark$

**17**

A garden centre sells three types of potato.

- First early potatoes, 12 varieties
- Second early potatoes, 8 varieties
- Main crop potatoes, 15 varieties

A gardener picks two varieties, one from each of the types of potato.
Each variety is equally likely to be picked.
How many ways can the gardener select two varieties?

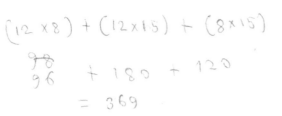

$(12 \times 8) + (12 \times 15) + (8 \times 15)$

$96 + 180 + 120$

$= 369$

**18**

A water meter measures the volume of water being used by a large factory.
The graph shows the number of litres used by the factory over several seconds.

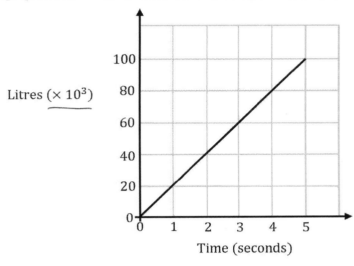

Litres ($\times 10^3$)

Time (seconds)

$5s = 100\,000$
$\times 12$
$60s = 1\,200\,000$

At this rate how many litres will the factory use in one minute?    $1,200,000$ ✓

**19**

Solid $A$ and solid $B$ are similar.
The length ratio of both solids is shown in the table.
Complete the table to show the ratios of the area and volumes of both solids.

|  | Solid $A$ : Solid $B$ | | |
|---|---|---|---|
| Length | 3 | : | 4 |
| Area | 9 | : | 16 |
| Volume | 27 | : | 64 |

✓

**20**

Find the roots of $(3x - 8)(7x + 4) = 0$     $x = -\frac{8}{3}$ or $\frac{4}{7}$  two   $\left(-\frac{8}{3}, 0\right)$ and $\left(\frac{4}{7}, 0\right)$

**21**

Prove $a + b - c = 180°$

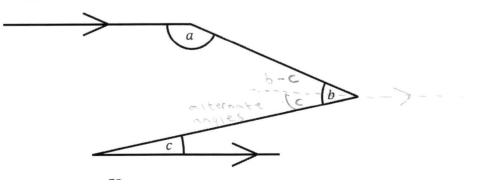

$a$

$b - c$

alternate angles

$c$

$b$

$c$

**22**

A social study on the weekly earnings of people living in the UK in 1971 was conducted.
The weekly earnings of 10 people are shown in £.

8    7    6    12    13    1    2    10    4    97

Calculate the mean, median and mode for these data giving a reason as to how suitable each average is.

*(handwritten)* 8+7+6    8+12 + 6+4 + 1+2+97 + 13+7 + 10

20 + 10  + 100 + 20 + 10 = 130+30 = £160

160/10 = £16   mean   suitable less skewed by extremes

£7.50 → median   suitable   unaffected by extremes

mode   not suitable   same ff few

$\frac{1}{2} \times$ x (a+b)

**23**

The points $P, Q, R$ and $S$ are shown on the axes below.
$QR$ and $PS$ are parallel.
The area of the trapezium $PQRS$ is 60 square units.
Work out possible coordinates for $P, Q, R$ and $S$.

*(handwritten)* QP × (QR = PS  PS − QR)

e.g.  Q (0,6)    R = (10,6)
      P (0,1)    S = (14,1)

$\frac{1}{2} \times (6-1) \times (10+24) = 6 cm 60$

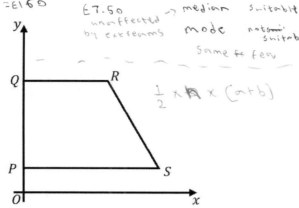

**24**

The table shows information on mean amount spent on grocery shopping each week for 120 people.
Draw a cumulative frequency graph for the data.

| Mean amount spent, £x | Frequency |
|---|---|
| $20 < x \le 50$ | 32 |
| $50 < x \le 60$ | 18 |
| $60 < x \le 80$ | 48 |
| $80 < x \le 110$ | 22 |

*(handwritten)* 50  98  110 X 120

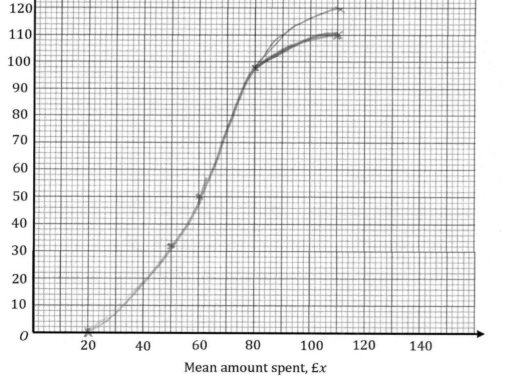

Cumulative frequency

Mean amount spent, £x

**25**

Find the interquartile range for the data shown in the cumulative frequency graph below. 20 ✓

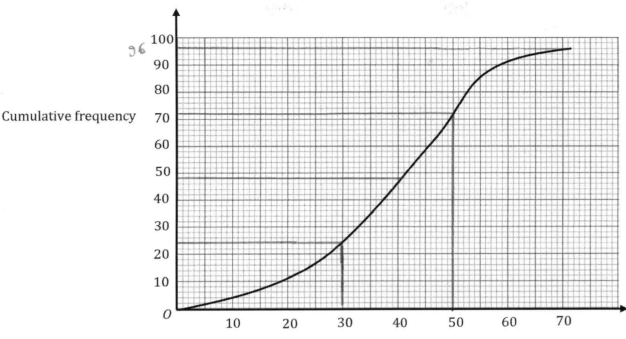

Cumulative frequency

Mean height of daffodils, $h$ cm

**26**

The equation of a curve is $y = (x + 4)^2 - 10$
Find the coordinates of the turning point.

$y = x^2 + 8x + 16 - 10$
$y = x^2 + 8x + 6$

$(-a, b)$ from $(x + a)^2 + b$

$(-4, -10)$

**27**

The diagram shows a cyclic quadrilateral.
$a : b = 7 : 8$
Find the ratio $a : c$

$7 + 8 = 15$

$a + b = 180°$       $180/15 = 12$

$12 \times 7 = 84$

$2a + c = 180$       $84 : 12$
$168 + c = 180$      $42 : 6$
$c = 12$             $21 : 3$
                     $7 : 1$ ✓

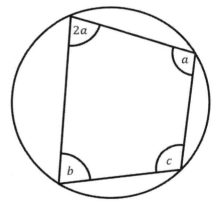

**28**

12 photocopiers work at the same rate.
The 12 photocopiers can copy 720 pages in one minute.
8 photocopiers operate for 2 minutes.
Then all the photocopiers operate until 1920 pages are copied.
How long were all 12 photocopiers working together? 2 min

$720/12 = 60$ p per min
$60 \times 8 = 480$     $480 \times 2 = 960$
$1920 - 480 = 1440$
$1920 - 960 = 960$
$960/720 = 1$ min     $1440/720 = 2$ min
                      20 sec

**29**

**(a)**

Convert $0.0\dot{8}$ into a simplified fraction.

$10x = 0.\dot{8}$
$100x = 8.\dot{8}$     $\frac{8}{90} = \frac{4}{45}$ ✓

**(b)**

Convert $2 \div 0.2\dot{7}$ into a simplified fraction.

$x = 0.2\dot{7}$   $10x = 2.\dot{7}$
$9x = 2.5$      $\frac{25}{90} = \frac{5}{18}$   55   $2 \div \frac{5}{18} = \frac{36}{5}$ ✓

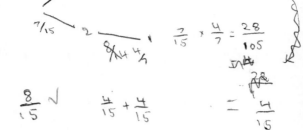 

**30**

15 coins are in a bag.

7 are £2 coins and the rest are £1 coins.

Two coins are selected without replacement.

Find the probability that the mean of the coins selected is £1.50.   $\frac{8}{15}$ ✓    $\frac{4}{15}+\frac{4}{15}$    $=\frac{4}{15}$

**31**

A and B are points on the circumference of the circle with centre O.

M is the midpoint of the straight line AB.

Find the equation of the circle.

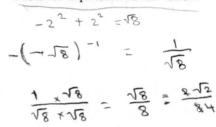 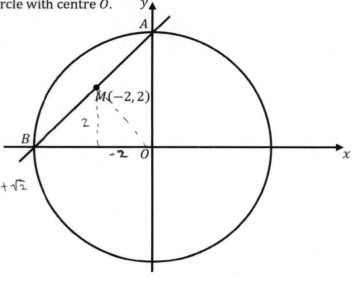

$-2^2 + 2^2 = \sqrt{8}$

$-(-\sqrt{8})^{-1} = \frac{1}{\sqrt{8}}$

$\frac{1}{\sqrt{8}} \times \frac{\sqrt{8}}{\sqrt{8}} = \frac{\sqrt{8}}{8} = \frac{2\sqrt{2}}{84}$

$y = \frac{\sqrt{2}}{4}x + c$         $y = \frac{\sqrt{2}}{4}x + 4 + \sqrt{2}$

$2 = \frac{\sqrt{2}}{4}(-2) + c$

$2 = -\frac{\sqrt{2}}{2} + c$

$4 = -\sqrt{2} + c$         $4 + \sqrt{2} = c$

**32**

The graph is a sketch of $y = \cos x$ for $-360° \le x \le 360°$

Find the coordinates of A and B.

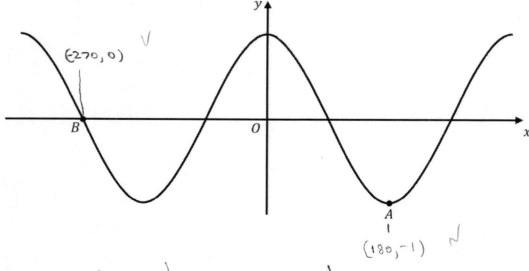

$(-270, 0)$ ✓

$A$

$(180, -1)$ ✓

**33**

**(a)**

Work out the value of $32^{-\frac{1}{5}}$    $\frac{1}{32^{\frac{1}{5}}}$    $2^5 = 32$    $\frac{1}{2}$ ✓

**(b)**

Write $32^{2x} \times \left(\frac{1}{4}\right)^{-2}$ as a power of 2 in terms of x.

# Paper 1 Higher: Practice Set 2 Solutions

**1**

$$\sqrt{3^4 + 12^2} = \sqrt{81 + 144}$$
$$= \sqrt{225}$$
$$= 15$$

**2**

Three billion is 3,000,000,000.
For standard form the start number must be between 1 and 10.
The power must be an integer.
The correct answer is $3 \times 10^9$

**3**

Raise each term in the brackets to the power of 4.
Use the law of indices: $(a^m)^n = a^{mn}$
$3^4 = 81$ and $(c^5)^4 = c^{20}$
Combine these terms to give the correct answer $81c^{20}$

**4**

$R = \frac{20}{A}$ is an example of inverse proportion and can be thought of as "$R$ is inversely proportional to $A$".
This means $A$ and $R$ will proportionally change in exactly opposite ways.
Increasing $A$ by 100% is the same as multiplying $A$ by 2.
The exact opposite to multiply by 2 is divide by 2.
$R$ will divide by 2.
In percentage terms, dividing by 2 is the same as decreasing by 50%.

**5**

$y^2 - 121$ is an example of the difference of two squares: $a^2 - b^2 = (a + b)(a - b)$
$y^2 - 121 = (y + 11)(y - 11)$

**6**

$9x + 7 \geq 5 + 4x$
$5x + 7 \geq 5$
$5x \geq -2$
$x \geq -\dfrac{2}{5}$

**7**

Both terms are raised to the same power (3) and can be combined as a single product raised to the same power (3):

$$\left(\sqrt{27}\right)^3 \times \left(\sqrt{3}\right)^3 = \left(\sqrt{27} \times \sqrt{3}\right)^3$$
$$= \left(\sqrt{81}\right)^3$$
$$= 9^3$$
$$= 729$$

```
      8   1
  ×       9
  ---------
  7   2   9
  ---------
```

**8**

The general formula for the area of a sector of angle $x$ is:
$$\text{area of sector} = \frac{x}{360} \times \pi r^2$$
$$= \frac{120}{360} \times \pi \times 9^2$$

57

$$= \frac{1}{3} \times \pi \times 81$$
$$= 27\pi$$

The correct answer is $27\pi$ cm$^2$.

### 9

If a whole number is rounded to the nearest 100 then:

      The last two digits of the smallest number must end in 50, e.g. 250
      The last two digits of the largest number must end in 49, e.g. 149

Multiply the mean by 5 to get the sum of the rounded numbers:

$80 \times 5 = 400$

For the maximum sum, each number must have been 49 units larger since this would have been "lost" due to rounding.

This happened five times, so add $49 \times 5 = 245$ to 400 to get the maximum possible sum of the original numbers:

$400 + 245 = 645$

The correct answer is 645.

### 10

The first integer is $n$.

For each consecutive integer add 1 unit to give the five consecutive integers:

$n, \qquad n+1, \qquad n+2, \qquad n+3, \qquad n+4$

The mean will be given by

$$\text{mean} = \frac{n+n+1+n+2+n+3+n+4}{5}$$
$$= \frac{5n+10}{5}$$
$$= n+2$$

The correct answer is $n + 2$

### 11(a)

The area of a parallelogram is the product of its base and the perpendicular height.
The base is $3a$ and the height is $2h$ so the area is $3a \times 2h = 6ah$

### 11(b)

Form a right-angled triangle to find the unknown side length (call this $x$) of the trapeziums.

$a : h = 2 : 3$

Use ratio cross multiply to find an equation containing $a$ and $h$:

$3a = 2h$

Use Pythagoras to find $x$:

$$x^2 = (3a)^2 + a^2$$
$$= 9a^2 + a^2$$
$$= 10a^2$$
$$x = \sqrt{10}a$$

Cross multiplying a ratio

$a : h$

$2 : 3$

$3a = 2h$

The perimeter of the parallelogram:

$$\text{perimeter} = 3a + 3a + \sqrt{10}a + \sqrt{10}a$$
$$= 6a + 2\sqrt{10}a$$

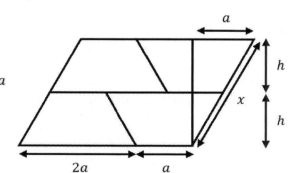

**12**

The probability that the bird observed was a house sparrow is equal to the proportion that the house sparrow sector makes of the pie chart.

The angles sum to 360°:

$$x + 70 + 3x - 10 + 2x = 360$$
$$6x + 60 = 360$$
$$6x = 300$$
$$x = 50$$

House sparrow: $2x = 100$

The correct probability is $\frac{100}{360}$ or $\frac{5}{18}$ if fully simplified.

**13**

$$\frac{0.848 \times 37.4^2}{\sqrt{109.34}} \approx \frac{0.8 \times 40^2}{\sqrt{100}}$$
$$\approx \frac{0.8 \times 1600}{10}$$
$$\approx 0.8 \times 160$$
$$\approx 128$$

$$40^2 = 40 \times 40$$
$$= 4 \times 10 \times 4 \times 10$$
$$= 16 \times 100$$
$$= 1600$$

$$0.8 \times 160 = 8 \times 16$$
$$= 128$$

**14**

$a : b = 3 : 11$ and $3(a + b) = 462$ [1]

Use ratio cross multiply to form an equation containing $a$ and $b$:

$$3b = 11a$$
$$b = \frac{11}{3}a$$

Substitute into [1]:
$$3(a + b) = 462$$
$$3\left(a + \frac{11}{3}a\right) = 462$$
$$3\left(\frac{14}{3}a\right) = 462$$
$$14a = 462$$
$$a = 33$$

$$b = \frac{11}{3} \times 33$$
$$= 121$$
$$3(a - b) = 3(33 - 121)$$
$$= 3(-88)$$
$$= -264$$

The correct answer is $-264$.

Cross multiplying a ratio

$$a : b$$

$$3 : 11$$
$$3b = 11a$$

$$\begin{array}{r} 3\phantom{.}\ 3 \\ 1\ 4\ \overline{\big)\ 4\ ^4 6\ ^4 2} \end{array}$$

**15**

The decagons (10-sided shapes) are congruent (identical).

$x$ will be formed from two exterior angles.

The exterior angle of a 10-sided shape is: $\frac{360}{10} = 36°$

$$x = 2 \times 36$$
$$= 72°$$

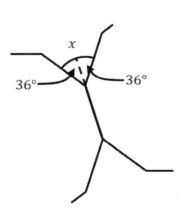

**16**

Use the product rule for counting to obtain the number of different ways of selecting three packets of seed. One item is being picked from each category of vegetables, fruit and herbs, so the numbers can be multiplied:

$25 \times 12 \times 8 = 2400$

There are 2400 different combinations.

**17**

There are three ways in which the required selection could be made:

      First early and second early

      First early and main crop

      Second early and main crop

Use the product rule for counting to obtain the number of different ways of selecting two varieties:

      First early and second early: $12 \times 8 = 96$

      First early and main crop: $12 \times 15 = 180$

      Second early and main crop: $8 \times 15 = 120$

Sum the totals to obtain the correct answer: $96 + 180 + 120 = 396$ different ways.

**18**

The graph is a straight line which means the rate of usage is constant.

The line starts at the origin, so the number of litres used is directly proportional to time.

At 5 seconds $100 \times 10^3$ litres of water have been used.

The factory will use 12 times this volume in one minute (since $\frac{60}{5} = 12$).

$$12 \times 100 \times 10^3 = 1200 \times 10^3$$
$$= 1.2 \times 10^6$$

The factory uses 1.2 million litres in one minute.

**19**

For similar shapes:

The area ratio is the square of the length ratio.

The volume ratio is the cube of the length ratio.

The completed table is shown.

|  | Solid $A$ : Solid $B$ | | |
|---|---|---|---|
| Length | 3 | : | 4 |
| Area | 9 | : | 16 |
| Volume | 27 | : | 64 |

**20**

The roots are the same as the solutions of the equation.

$(3x - 8)(7x + 4) = 0$

| $3x - 8 = 0$ | $7x + 4 = 0$ |
|---|---|
| $3x = 8$ | $7x = -4$ |
| $x = \dfrac{8}{3}$ | $x = -\dfrac{4}{7}$ |

The roots are $\frac{8}{3}$ and $-\frac{4}{7}$.

**21**

Two of the lines shown are parallel.

A third parallel line can be added that passes through the angle at $b$.

Part of this angle is allied to $a$ and the other part is alternate to $c$.

The parts that make up angle $b$ are $c$ and $b - c$ as shown.

Using allied angles: $a + b - c = 180°$

This completes the proof.

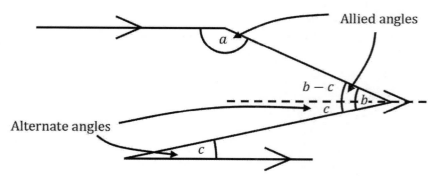

60

**22**

Mean:

$$\frac{8 + 7 + 6 + 12 + 13 + 1 + 2 + 10 + 4 + 97}{10} = \frac{160}{10}$$
$$= 16$$

Not suitable as the mean is affected by extreme values such as 97.
The mean is not suitable when the majority of the data are either less than or more than the mean.

Median:
In ascending order: 1, 2, 4, 6, 7, 8, 10, 12, 13, 97.
There are 10 values, so the median is between the 5th and 6th terms: 7.5
Suitable since it represents a more typical value and is unaffected by extreme values.

Mode:
All the numbers occur exactly once.
Unsuitable since all numbers occur equally frequently.

**23**

The area of a trapezium is given by:
area $= \frac{1}{2}h(a + b)$ where $h = PQ$, $a = QR$ and $b = PS$
There are infinite solutions to this question, but all answers must satisfy fundamental criteria:
- $P$ and $Q$ must have 0 for their $x$-coordinate
- $Q$ and $R$ have the same $y$-coordinate with $y > 0$
- $P$ and $S$ have the same $y$-coordinate with $y > 0$
- $QR < PS$

Here is a suitable solution:

$PQ = 5,$     $PS = 14,$     $QR = 10,$     so   $\frac{1}{2} \times 5 \times (10 + 14) = 60$

$P(0, 1),$     $S(14,1),$     $Q(0,6),$     $R(10,6)$

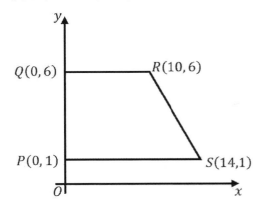

**24**

Draw another column on the right of the table labelled cumulative frequency.
Then plot the upper value of the mean amount spent inequality against the cumulative frequency value.
Note that nobody spent less than £20 so we also plot a point at (20, 0)

| Mean amount spent, £$x$ | Frequency | Cumulative frequency |
|---|---|---|
| $20 < x \leq 50$ | 32 | 32 |
| $50 < x \leq 60$ | 18 | 50 |
| $60 < x \leq 80$ | 48 | 98 |
| $80 < x \leq 110$ | 22 | 120 |

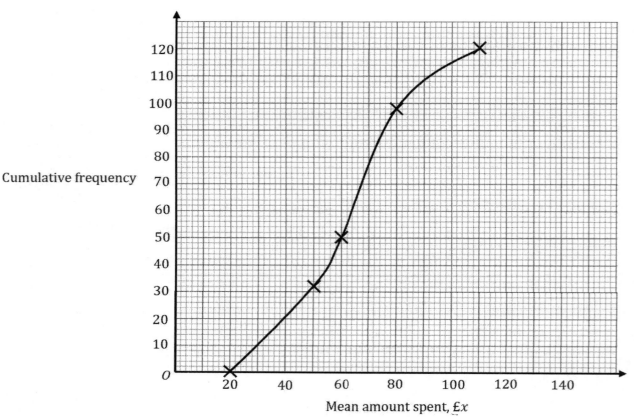

**25**

The maximum frequency reached by the curve is 96.

The lower quartile is reached at $\frac{1}{4}$ of the total cumulative frequency: $96 \times \frac{1}{4} = 24$

Draw a horizontal line from 24 across to the curve, this corresponds to a value of 30.

The upper quartile is reached at $\frac{3}{4}$ of the total cumulative frequency: $96 \times \frac{3}{4} = 72$

Draw a horizontal line from 72 across to the curve, this corresponds to a value of 50.

The interquartile range is the difference in the quartiles: $50 - 30 = 20$

The interquartile range is 20.

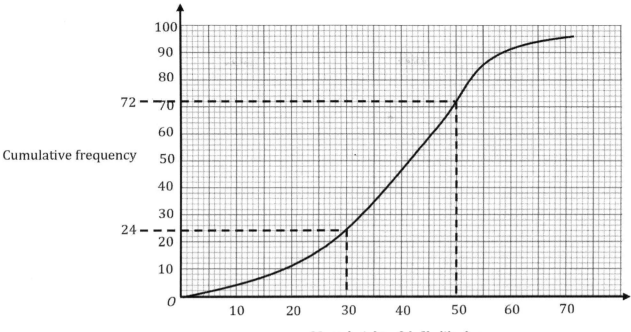

Cumulative frequency

Mean height of daffodils, $h$cm

## 26
An equation of the form $y = (x + a)^2 + b$ has a turning point at $(-a, b)$
For $y = (x + 4)^2 - 10$ the turning point is located at $(-4, -10)$

## 27
The opposite angles in a cyclic quadrilateral sum to $180°$.
$2a + c = 180$ and $a + b = 180$
The sum of $a + b$ is known and the ratio $a : b = 7 : 8$ is known.
Divide 180 into the ratio $7 : 8$ to find $a$ and $b$ (only $a$ is required for this question):
$180 \times \dfrac{7}{15} = 84$,     $180 \times \dfrac{8}{15} = 96$
$a = 84$ and $b = 96$
$2(84) + c = 180$
$168 + c = 180$
$c = 12$
$a : c = 84 : 12$
$= 7 : 1$

## 28
This is a variation question.
Photocopiers and pages are directly proportional (they will vary in identical proportions).
Pages and time are directly proportional (they will vary in identical proportions).
Photocopiers and time are inversely proportional (they will vary in opposite proportions).
12 photocopiers copy 720 pages in one minute.
12 photocopiers will copy 1440 pages in 2 minutes (pages $\times$ 2 and time $\times$ 2).
8 photocopiers will copy 960 pages in 2 minutes (photocopiers $\times \frac{2}{3}$ and pages $\times \frac{2}{3}$).
There are $1920 - 960 = 960$ pages remaining.
12 photocopiers will copy 960 pages in 1 minute and 20 seconds (photocopiers $\times \frac{3}{2}$ and time $\div \frac{3}{2}$).
The correct answer is 1 minute and 20 seconds or 80 seconds.

| Photocopiers | Pages | Time (mins) |
|---|---|---|
| 12 | 720 | 1 |
| 12 | 1440 | 2 |
| 8 | 960 | 2 |
| 12 | 960 | $\frac{4}{3}$ |

Photocopiers: $\times \frac{2}{3}$ (12 to 12), $\times \frac{3}{2}$ (8 to 12)

Pages: $\times 2$ (720 to 1440), $\times \frac{2}{3}$ (1440 to 960)

Time: $\times 2$ (1 to 2), $\div \frac{3}{2}$ (2 to $\frac{4}{3}$)

**29(a)**

$$x = 0.0\dot{8}$$
$$10x = 0.\dot{8} \quad [1]$$
$$100x = 8.\dot{8} \quad [2]$$
$$[2] - [1]$$
$$90x = 8$$
$$x = \frac{8}{90}$$
$$= \frac{4}{45}$$

**29(b)**

$$x = 0.2\dot{7}$$
$$10x = 2.\dot{7} \quad [1]$$
$$100x = 27.\dot{7} \quad [2]$$
$$[2] - [1]$$
$$90x = 25$$
$$x = \frac{25}{90}$$
$$= \frac{5}{18}$$

$$2 \div 0.2\dot{7} = 2 \div \frac{5}{18}$$
$$= 2 \times \frac{18}{5}$$
$$= \frac{36}{5}$$
$$= 7\frac{1}{5}$$

**30**

There are $15 - 7 = 8$ £1 coins.

If two coins are selected with a mean of £1.50 then the total value of the coins selected was £3.

Either a £2 and a £1 or a £1 and a £2 were selected.

This is shown as two pathways on a probability tree:

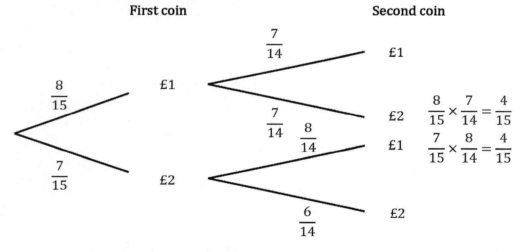

**First coin**    **Second coin**

$\frac{8}{15}$ → £1 ; $\frac{7}{14}$ → £1 ; $\frac{7}{14}$ → £2 : $\frac{8}{15} \times \frac{7}{14} = \frac{4}{15}$

$\frac{7}{15}$ → £2 ; $\frac{8}{14}$ → £1 : $\frac{7}{15} \times \frac{8}{14} = \frac{4}{15}$ ; $\frac{6}{14}$ → £2

Note that $\frac{7}{14} = \frac{1}{2}$

Add the probabilities to get the answer: $\frac{4}{15} + \frac{4}{15} = \frac{8}{15}$

The probability that the mean of the coins selected is £1.50 is $\frac{8}{15}$.

**31**

The general equation of a circle with centre $O$ is $x^2 + y^2 = r^2$

$A$ is on the $y$-axis so its $x$-coordinate is zero.

64

The $y$-coordinate of $M$, 2, represents half the unit distance to $A$ since it is a midpoint.
This means that $A$ has a $y$-coordinate of 4 (or by the same conclusion $B$ has an $x$-coordinate of $-4$).
The radius of the circle is 4 so the equation of the circle is $x^2 + y^2 = 16$

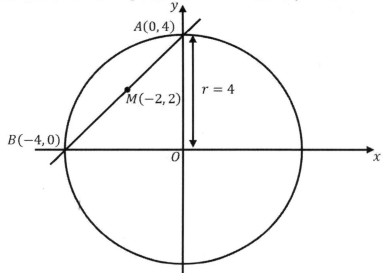

**32**

This is a standard cosine curve which is symmetrical about the $y$-axis.
The cosine graph repeats every $360°$ and is contained between $-1$ and $1$.
Point $A$ is $(180°, -1)$ and point $B$ is $(-270°, 0)$

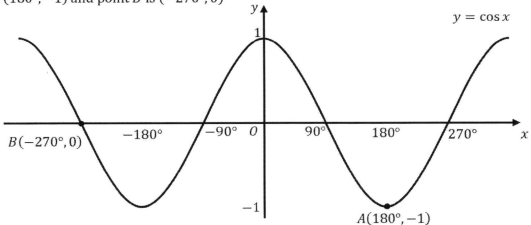

**33(a)**

$$32^{-\frac{1}{5}} = \frac{1}{32^{\frac{1}{5}}}$$
$$= \frac{1}{2}$$

A negative power can be written as a reciprocal with a positive power:

e.g. $\left(\frac{a}{3}\right)^{-2} = \left(\frac{3}{a}\right)^{2}$

$\frac{1}{5}$ as a power is the fifth root.

**33(b)**

$$32^{2x} \times \left(\frac{1}{4}\right)^{-2} = (2^5)^{2x} \times (4^{-1})^{-2}$$
$$= 2^{10x} \times 4^2$$
$$= 2^{10x} \times (2^2)^2$$
$$= 2^{10x} \times 2^4$$
$$= 2^{10x+4}$$

$32 = 2^5$
$4 = 2^2$

# Paper 2 Higher: Practice Set 2

**1**
Convert 4.4375 into a simplified fraction.
Circle your answer.

$$\frac{55}{16} \qquad \frac{71}{16} \qquad \frac{35}{8} \qquad \frac{355}{8}$$

**2**
What is 300 as a percentage of 24?
Circle your answer.

$$8\% \qquad 1250\% \qquad 276\% \qquad 12.5\%$$

**3**
Which of the following coordinates lie on the curve $y = x^2 + 3$?
Circle any answers.

$$\left(\frac{1}{2}, \frac{13}{4}\right) \qquad (6, 15) \qquad (-2, -1) \qquad \left(-\frac{3}{2}, \frac{21}{4}\right)$$

**4**
Using the units
g        kg        cm$^3$        m$^3$
write down two units of density.

**5**
The graph shows the density and volume of metals with the same mass.
The mass of each metal is 800g.
Complete the graph.

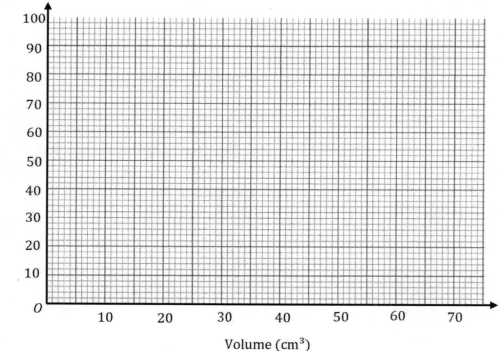

**6**

Solve $5(2x + 7) = 12 + 56x$

**7**

The diagram shows a triangular prism with volume 96 cm³.
The base of the triangular cross section is $b$ cm.
Find the value of $b$.

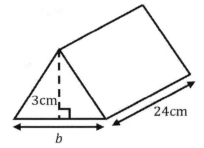

3cm

24cm

$b$

**8**

Describe fully the single transformation that maps triangle A to triangle B.

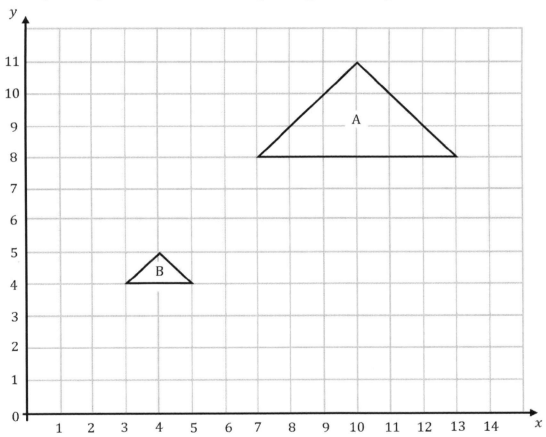

**9**

The table shows information about the percentage spend on health by 80 countries.

| Percentage spend, $x\%$ | Frequency |
|---|---|
| $0 < x \leq 5$ | 18 |
| $5 < x \leq 10$ | 27 |
| $10 < x \leq 20$ | 26 |
| $20 < x \leq 30$ | 9 |

Work out an estimate for the mean percentage spend on health.

**10**

Work out the size of angle $x$.

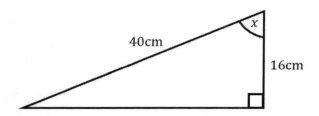

40cm

16cm

**11**

Work out the next term in this quadratic sequence.

17          23          32          44          ...

**12**

Simplify the expression     $\dfrac{45x^2}{18x + 27x^2}$

**13**

The table shows the population of two countries and the number of doctors in each country.
Show that country B has about twice as many people per doctor than country A.

| Country | Population | Number of doctors |
|---------|-----------|-------------------|
| A | 116 000 000 | 88 000 |
| B | 78 000 000 | 30 000 |

**14**

Two straight lines intersect at point $R$.
Find the coordinates of $R$.

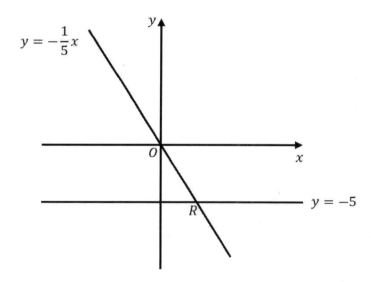

$y = -\dfrac{1}{5}x$

$y = -5$

**15**

A candle is burning.
Every hour the brightness of the candlelight decreases by one third.
Initially the candle has brightness $b$ units.
What will the brightness be in two hours in terms of $b$?

**16**

£5000 is invested in a bank account that pays 1.8% compound interest.
Determine whether it is possible to earn £1500 in interest over 15 years?

**17**

A glacier is melting.
A model predicts that the glacier loses 5% of its mass at the start of the year every year.
The glacier has a mass of $1 \times 10^8$ tonnes.
Two years later the glacier has a mass of $9 \times 10^7$ tonnes.
Is this more or less than expected?

**18**

**(a)**
Factorise fully $16x^2 - 4$

**(b)**
Factorise $5x^2 - 29x - 42$

**19**
Work out the area of this parallelogram.

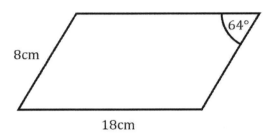

**20**
**(a)**
Use set notation to identify the shaded region.

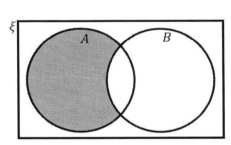

**(b)**
Use set notation to identify the shaded region.

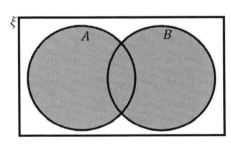

**21**
The sum of the lengths of the parallel sides in the trapezium is six times the height of the trapezium.
The area of the trapezium is $768\text{cm}^2$.
Find the height of the trapezium.

**22**

The energy $E$ of an electronic component is directly proportional to the square of the charge $Q$.
When $E = 40, Q = 20$ and $Q \geq 0$
The maximum value of $E$ is 250.
What value will $Q$ take at this time?

**23**

**(a)**

The graph shows a sketch of $y = x^2$
A student is using a graphical method to solve $x^2 - 2x - 3 = 0$
By drawing a straight line complete the method.

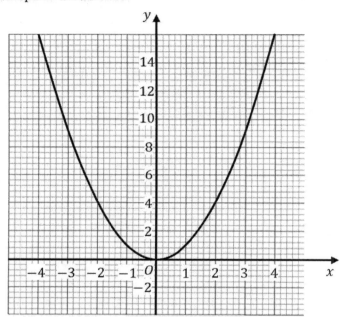

**(b)**

Here is the method used by a student to solve the equation $3x^2 + 4 = 2x + 4$

$3x^2 + 4 = 2x + 4$

$3x^2 = 2x$      Subtract 4 from both sides

$3x = 2$      Divide both sides by $x$

$x = \dfrac{2}{3}$      Divide both sides by 3

Is this the correct method?
Explain your answer.

**24**

The cross section of a template is shown below.
The template is made from two similar trapeziums.
$EF = 14.4$cm
What fraction of $ABCD$ is the shaded area?

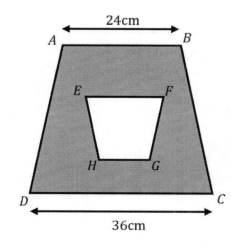

**25**

**(a)**

The histogram shows information about the amount spent at a supermarket.

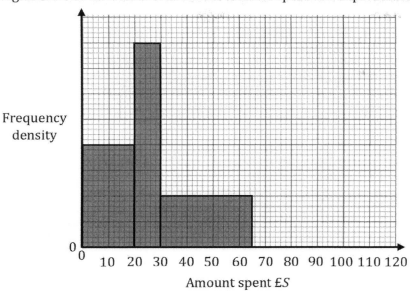

There are 16 people where $S < 20$
There are 66 people where $65 \leq S < 120$
No one spent more than £120.
Complete the histogram including the frequency density scale.

**(b)**

The histogram shows the monthly spend on gas bills.

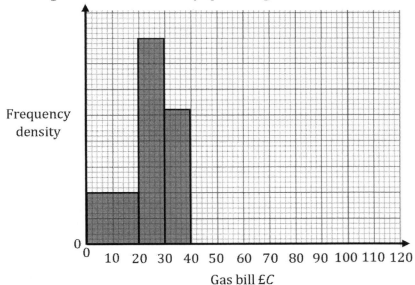

There are 10 people with $C < 20$
There are 30 people with $40 \leq C < 90$
There are 45 people with $90 \leq C < 120$
How many people are represented on the histogram?

71

**26**

Two go karts are in a race.

Go kart A accelerated constantly for the first 8 seconds reaching a speed of 10m/s and then continued at a constant speed until the race was completed 16 seconds later.

Go kart B accelerated constantly for the first 4 seconds reaching a speed of 9m/s and then continued at a constant speed until the race was completed.

Which go kart won the race?

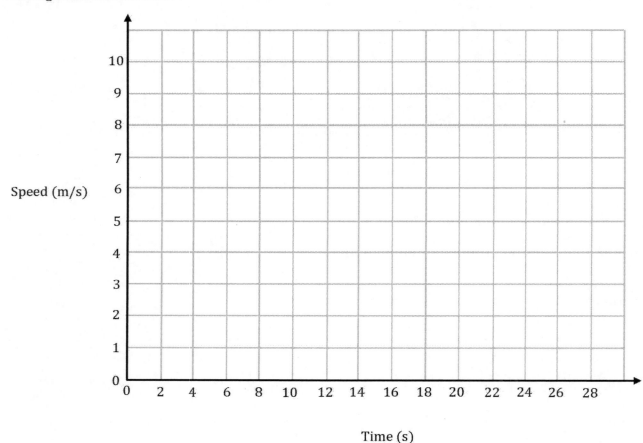

Time (s)

**27**

$$pressure = \frac{force}{area}$$

A platform can take a maximum safe pressure of $100N/m^2$.
The platform is in the shape of a rectangle.
Each measurement is correct to the nearest 10cm.
A force of 4000 newtons is applied to the platform.
The force is correct to the nearest 50 newtons.
Is the platform pressure safe?

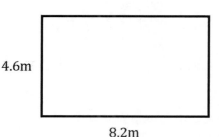

4.6m

8.2m

**28**

Solve $\dfrac{x}{5} + \dfrac{6x}{x+3} = 1$

Give your solutions to three significant figures.

**29**

*ABCDE* is a pentagon.

Show that *BCDE* is not a trapezium.

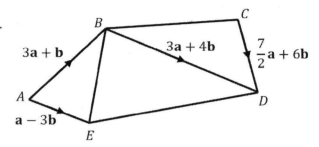

## Paper 2 Higher: Practice Set 2 Solutions

**1**

Type 4.4375 into the calculator to obtain the correct answer: $\frac{71}{16}$

**2**

$$\frac{300}{24} \times 100 = 1250\%$$

**3**

Substitute the $x$-coordinate of each option into the equation $y = x^2 + 3$
If the $y$ value is the same as the given $y$-coordinate then the point lies on the curve.

$$y = \left(\frac{1}{2}\right)^2 + 3 \qquad y = 6^2 + 3 \qquad y = (-2)^2 + 3 \qquad y = \left(-\frac{3}{2}\right)^2 + 3$$
$$= \frac{13}{4} \qquad\qquad\quad = 39 \qquad\qquad = 7 \qquad\qquad\qquad = \frac{21}{4}$$

$\left(\frac{1}{2}, \frac{13}{4}\right)$ and $\left(-\frac{3}{2}, \frac{21}{4}\right)$ both lie on the curve.

**4**

The formula for density is density $= \frac{\text{mass}}{\text{volume}}$

Any unit written as a mass/volume will be acceptable:
$g/cm^3$, $g/m^3$, $kg/cm^3$ or $kg/m^3$ are all correct.

**5**

density $= \dfrac{\text{mass}}{\text{volume}}$

mass $=$ density $\times$ volume

The mass is given as 800g.

To plot the graph, select any coordinate pairing with a product of 800.

The curve formed is a reciprocal graph (inverse proportion).

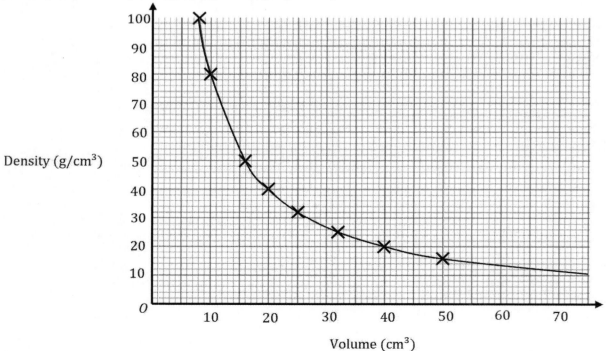

**6**

$5(2x + 7) = 12 + 56x$

$10x + 35 = 12 + 56x$

$35 = 12 + 46x$

$23 = 46x$

$x = \dfrac{1}{2}$

**7**

Use the general volume of a prism formula:

Volume of a prism = cross-sectional area × depth

$b = \dfrac{8}{3}$

$\dfrac{1}{2} \times$ base × height × depth = 96

$\dfrac{1}{2} \times b \times 3 \times 24 = 96$

$36b = 96$

$b = \dfrac{8}{3}$

**8**

The triangles are orientated in the same direction but the size of each triangle is different.

This means the transformation is an enlargement.

Use the ratio of the base lengths of each triangle to find the scale factor.

Triangle B has base 2 units and triangle A has base 6 units.

The scale factor of the enlargement is $\dfrac{2}{6} = \dfrac{1}{3}$

Join the corresponding points of the triangles together and project the lines until they intersect.

The intersection point is the centre of the enlargement: $(1, 2)$

The correct answer: enlargement scale factor $\dfrac{1}{3}$ centre $(1, 2)$

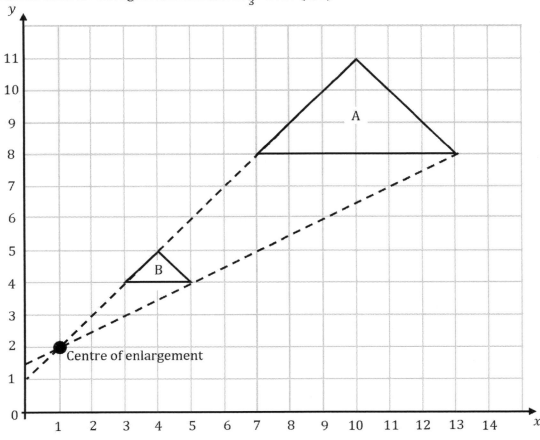

**9**

This is a grouped frequency table.
Use midpoints to estimate the mean.
Add two columns to the table, one for midpoints and the other for midpoint × frequency.

| Percentage spend, $x\%$ | Frequency | Midpoints | Midpoint × Frequency |
|---|---|---|---|
| $0 < x \le 5$ | 18 | 2.5 | $18 \times 2.5 = 45$ |
| $5 < x \le 10$ | 27 | 7.5 | $27 \times 7.5 = 202.5$ |
| $10 < x \le 20$ | 26 | 15 | $26 \times 15 = 390$ |
| $20 < x \le 30$ | 9 | 25 | $9 \times 25 = 225$ |

Sum the final column and divide by the frequency total (80):

$$\text{mean} = \frac{45 + 202.5 + 390 + 225}{80}$$
$$= 10.78125$$

The mean estimate for percentage spend on health is 10.78125%

**10**

Use SOH**CAH**TOA

With respect to $x$, the adjacent is 16 and the hypotenuse is 40.

$$\cos x = \frac{\text{adjacent}}{\text{hypotenuse}}$$
$$= \frac{16}{40}$$
$$x = \cos^{-1}\frac{16}{40}$$
$$= 66.4° \text{ (1dp)}$$

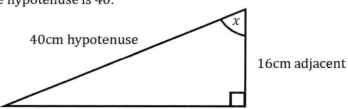

40cm hypotenuse

16cm adjacent

**11**

Find the first and second differences.
Continue the sequence to generate the next term of 59.

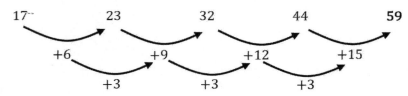

**12**

$$\frac{45x^2}{18x + 27x^2} = \frac{45x^2}{9x(2 + 3x)}$$
$$= \frac{5x}{2 + 3x}$$

Cancel out the common factor of $9x$.

**13**

People per doctor is calculated by dividing the number of people by the number of doctors for each country:

Country A: $\frac{116\,000\,000}{88\,000} \approx 1318$

Country B: $\frac{78\,000\,000}{30\,000} = 2600$

$2 \times 1318 \approx 2600$ so there are about twice as many people per doctor in country B.

**14**

$R$ lies on the line $y = -\frac{1}{5}x$

The $y$-coordinate of $R$ is $-5$.

The $x$-coordinate is found by substituting $y = -5$ into the equation $y = -\frac{1}{5}x$

$$-\frac{1}{5}x = -5$$
$$x = 25$$

The coordinates of $R$ are $(25, -5)$

**15**

If the brightness decreases by $\frac{1}{3}$ then the brightness after each hour will be $\frac{2}{3}$ what it was 1 hour ago.

This multiplier will be applied for each successive hour the candle burns.

In two hours the brightness, in terms of $b$, is:

$$\text{brightness} = \frac{2}{3} \times \frac{2}{3} \times b$$
$$= \frac{4}{9}b$$

The correct answer is $\frac{4}{9}b$

**16**

The general formula to calculate the value of an investment £$P$ at a compound interest rate of $r\%$ over $n$ years is:

$$\text{value of investment} = P\left(1 + \frac{r}{100}\right)^n$$

For the given information:

$$\text{value of investment} = 5000\left(1 + \frac{1.8}{100}\right)^{15}$$
$$= 6534.11$$

The interest earned is the difference between the original value invested and the current value.

$6534.11 - 5000 = 1534.11$

It is possible to earn more than £1500 in interest over 15 years at 1.8% compound interest.

**17**

The multiplier for a 5% decrease is 0.95.

The mass of the glacier after two years will be $1 \times 10^8 \times 0.95^2 = 9.025 \times 10^7$ tonnes.

The glacier has a mass which is less than the expected value of $9.025 \times 10^7$ tonnes.

**18(a)**

$$16x^2 - 4 = 4(4x^2 - 1)$$
$$= 4(2x + 1)(2x - 1) \qquad \text{Note difference of two squares}$$

**18(b)**

Multiply 5 by $-42$ to give $-210$.

Write a notional factorisation $(5x + \cdots)(5x + \cdots)$

Find a factor pair of $-210$ that sum to $-29$.

These factors are $-35$ and $6$.

Write the notional factorisation: $(5x + 6)(5x - 35)$

Divide any factors out of the brackets to form the correct factorisation (5 is a factor in $5x - 35$):

$$5x^2 - 29x - 42 = (5x + 6)(x - 7)$$

**19**

Opposite sides are equal in length in a parallelogram.
Use the base length of 18cm and then find the perpendicular height using trigonometry:

$$\sin 64° = \frac{\text{opposite}}{\text{hypotenuse}}$$

$$= \frac{h}{8}$$

$h = 8\sin 64°$

Now use the parallelogram area formula:
area = base × perpendicular height

$$= 18 \times 8\sin 64°$$

$$= 129.4\text{cm}^2 \text{ (1dp)}$$

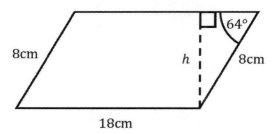

**20(a)**

Only part of $A$ is shaded: $A$ and not $B$.
The region is $A \cap B'$

**20(b)**

Both $A$ and $B$ are shaded: the sets have been unified, $A$ or $B$ or both.
The region is $A \cup B$

**21**

The area of a trapezium is given by:

$$\text{area of trapezium} = \frac{1}{2} \times \text{height} \times \text{sum of parallel sides}$$

This is an alternative way of stating $\frac{1}{2}h(a+b)$

Let the height be $h$.
The sum of the parallel sides will be $6h$.

$$\frac{1}{2} \times h \times 6h = 768$$

$$3h^2 = 768$$

$$h^2 = 256$$

$$h = 16$$

The trapezium has a height of 16cm.

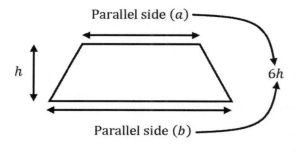

**22**

$E \propto Q^2$

$E = kQ^2$

Substitute the given values $E = 40$ and $Q = 20$ into the equation and solve for $k$:

$40 = k \times 20^2$

$40 = 400k$

$k = 0.1$

$E = 0.1Q^2$

Substitute $E = 250$ into the equation to find $Q$:

$250 = 0.1Q^2$

$2500 = Q^2$

$Q = 50$

The charge is 50 since $Q$ cannot be negative (the square root of 2500 is also $-50$).

**23(a)**

Notice $x^2$ appears in the equation $x^2 - 2x - 3 = 0$
Isolate the $x^2$ term: $x^2 = 2x + 3$

The expression on the right-hand side of this equation is the required graph equation.
Sketch the graph of $y = 2x + 3$ by picking two coordinates.
When $x = 4, y = 11$ and when $x = -2, y = -1$
Join the coordinates $(4, 11)$ and $(-2, -1)$ together.
The curve and the line intersect at the points where $x = -1$ and where $x = 3$
The solutions are $x = -1$ and $x = 3$

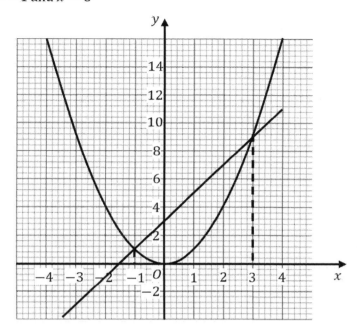

**23(b)**
The student has not used the correct method.
The student should not divide through by $x$ as this eliminates one of the solutions: $x = 0$
Factorising is the correct method:

$$3x^2 + 4 = 2x + 4$$
$$3x^2 = 2x \qquad \text{Subtract 4 from both sides.}$$
$$3x^2 - 2x = 0 \qquad \text{Subtract } 2x \text{ from both sides.}$$
$$x(3x - 2) = 0 \qquad \text{Factorise.}$$
$$x = 0 \text{ or } x = \frac{2}{3}$$

There are two solutions.

**24**
The shaded area is found by subtracting the small trapezium area from the large trapezium area.
However, this method would not be possible as there is no way of determining the heights of the trapeziums.
The correct method uses scale factors.
The sides $EF$ and $CD$ both correspond to each other as they represent the similar sides.
Use these sides to establish the length ratio:
$$EF : CD = 14.4 : 36$$
$$= 2 : 5$$
Square the length ratios to get the area ratios:
small trapezium area : large trapezium area $= 4 : 25$
The small trapezium represents $\frac{4}{25}$ of the area of the large trapezium.
The shaded area represents the remainder: $\frac{21}{25}$.

**25(a)**

The frequency of each interval on a histogram is represented by the area of each rectangle.

There is no scale on the frequency density axis.

The first rectangle $(0 < S < 20)$ has an area of 16.

Let the unknown length of this rectangle (the missing value on the frequency density axis) be $x$.

$20x = 16$

$\quad x = 0.8$

Use this to complete the frequency density axis, which is in increments of 0.2.

Let the unknown height of the rectangle defining $(65 < S < 120)$ be $y$:

$55y = 66$

$\quad y = 1.2$

Now complete the histogram.

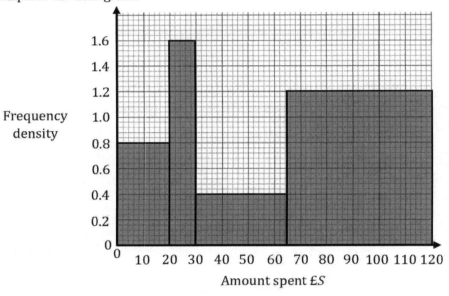

Amount spent £$S$

**25(b)**

The frequency of each interval on a histogram is represented by the area of each rectangle.

There is no scale on the frequency density axis.

The first rectangle $(0 < C < 20)$ has an area of 10.

Let the unknown length of this rectangle be $x$:

$20x = 10$

$\quad x = 0.5$

Use this to complete the frequency density axis, which is in increments of 0.25.

Now find the areas (frequencies) of the two other given rectangles.

$2 \times 10 = 20$ and $1.3 \times 10 = 13$

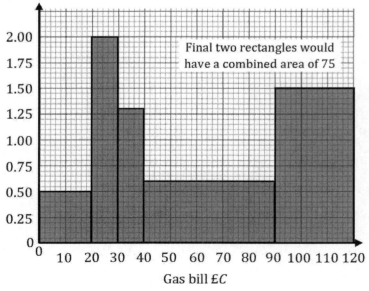

Final two rectangles would have a combined area of 75

Frequency density

Sum all of the frequencies together:

$10 + 20 + 13 + 30 + 45 = 118$

There are 118 people represented on the histogram.

Gas bill £$C$

**26**

The go kart that wins will have travelled the total race distance in the shortest time.

For go kart A:

Draw a straight line from the origin to the point $(8, 10)$

Constant acceleration is a straight line.

Draw a horizontal line from $(8, 10)$ to $(24, 10)$

Constant speed is a horizontal line.

Find the area under the graph for go kart A (this is the distance travelled):

area = triangle + rectangle
$$= \frac{1}{2} \times 8 \times 10 + 16 \times 10$$
$$= 200$$

The race was 200 metres.

For go kart B:

Draw a straight line from the origin to the point $(4, 9)$

Draw a horizontal line from $(4, 9)$ to $(24, 9)$

Find the area under the graph for go kart B:

area = triangle + rectangle
$$= \frac{1}{2} \times 4 \times 9 + 20 \times 9$$
$$= 198$$

At the time when go kart A finished, go kart B had travelled 198m, which was 2m behind.

This means that go kart A finished first.

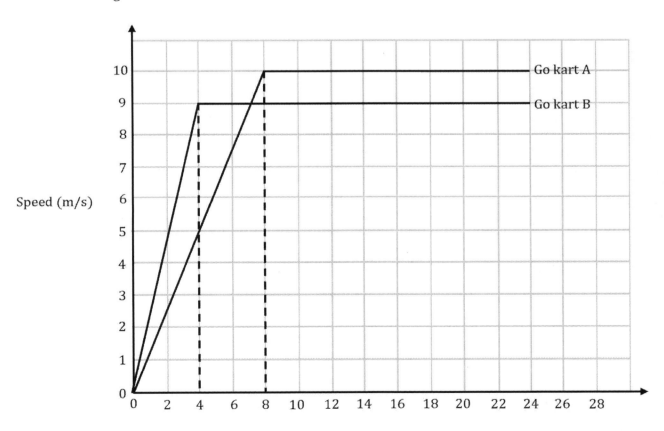

**27**

Find the error intervals for the width and length of the rectangle.

If each measurement is given to the nearest 10cm then there is an error of $\pm 5$cm on each measurement.

The error intervals in metres are:

$4.55 \leq$ width $< 4.65$ and $8.15 \leq$ length $< 8.25$

The force is given correct to the nearest 50 newtons, so there is an error of $\pm 25$ newtons on the force measurement.

The error interval for the force is:

$3975 \leq$ force $< 4025$

Find the error interval for the area of the rectangle:

$4.55 \times 8.15 \leq$ area $< 4.65 \times 8.25$

$37.0825 \leq$ area $< 38.3625$

Find the lower bound for the pressure:

$$\text{lower pressure bound} = \frac{\text{lower bound force}}{\text{upper bound area}}$$

$$= \frac{3975}{38.3625}$$

$$= 103.6 \ldots$$

Since the lower bound already exceeds the safe pressure limit of $100\text{N/m}^2$ we conclude that the platform is not safe.

**28**

$$\frac{x}{5} + \frac{6x}{x+3} = 1 \qquad \text{Multiply by 5.}$$

Multiply by $(x+3)$

$$x + \frac{30x}{x+3} = 5 \qquad \text{Expand the brackets.}$$

Collect the terms.

$$x(x+3) + 30x = 5(x+3) \qquad \text{Use the quadratic formula since the question said give}$$

$$x^2 + 3x + 30x = 5x + 15 \qquad \text{answers to 3sf (no point trying to factorise).}$$

$$x^2 + 28x - 15 = 0$$

Use the quadratic formula with $a = 1$, $b = 28$ and $c = -15$

$$x = \frac{-b \pm \sqrt{b^2 - 4ac}}{2a}$$

$$= \frac{-28 \pm \sqrt{28^2 - 4(1)(-15)}}{2(1)}$$

$$x = 0.526$$

$$x = -28.5$$

**29**

$BCDE$ is not a trapezium if it has no pairing of sides that are parallel.

In vector terms, parallel means vectors for the sides are scalar multiples of each other.

$$\overrightarrow{BE} = \overrightarrow{BA} + \overrightarrow{AE} \qquad \overrightarrow{BC} = \overrightarrow{BD} + \overrightarrow{DC} \qquad \overrightarrow{DE} = \overrightarrow{DB} + \overrightarrow{BE} \qquad \overrightarrow{CD} = \frac{7}{2}\mathbf{a} + 6\mathbf{b}$$

$$= -3\mathbf{a} - \mathbf{b} + \mathbf{a} - 3\mathbf{b} \qquad = 3\mathbf{a} + 4\mathbf{b} - \frac{7}{2}\mathbf{a} - 6\mathbf{b} \qquad = -3\mathbf{a} - 4\mathbf{b} - 2\mathbf{a} - 4\mathbf{b}$$

$$= -2\mathbf{a} - 4\mathbf{b} \qquad = -\frac{1}{2}\mathbf{a} - 2\mathbf{b} \qquad = -5\mathbf{a} - 8\mathbf{b}$$

None of the vectors for the four sides of $BCDE$ are scalar multiples of each other.

This means none of the sides are parallel, so $BCDE$ is not a trapezium (a trapezium has one pair of parallel sides).

## Paper 3 Higher: Practice Set 2

**1**

Circle the inequality shown by the diagram.

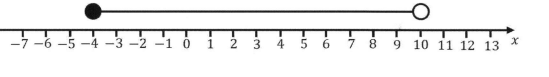

$-4 < x < 10$        $-4 < x \leq 10$        $-4 \leq x \leq 10$        $-4 \leq x < 10$

**2**

$y$ is 200% more than $x$.

Circle the simplified ratio $x : y$

    $1 : 300$          $1 : 200$          $1 : 3$          $1 : 2$

**3**

The first four terms of a linear sequence are    $-8$    $-2$    4    10

Circle the expression for the $n$th term of the sequence.

    $6n + 14$          $-6n + 14$          $-6n - 14$          $6n - 14$

**4**

Circle the equation of the line parallel to the $x$-axis.

    $y = -0.5$          $x = 0$          $x = 4$          $x = 2y$

**5**

Multiply out and simplify $(x - 12)^2$

**6**

Write 561 as the sum of a square number and a cube number.

**7**

The table shows the running times of 60 films.
Which time interval contains the median?

| Time, $t$ minutes | Number of films |
|---|---|
| $60 < t \leq 90$ | 7 |
| $90 < t \leq 110$ | 15 |
| $110 < t \leq 140$ | 13 |
| $140 < t \leq 180$ | 25 |

**8**

Use consistent metric units to complete the table.

| Length | Area | Volume | Perimeter |
|---|---|---|---|
| m | | | |

83

**9**

Rearrange $s = 0.5(u + v)t$ to make $v$ the subject.

**10**

$ACDE$ is a parallelogram.
$BE = BD$
Find the value of $x$.

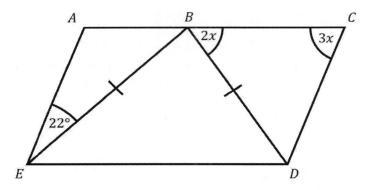

**11**

Hamilton and Navier are two towns.
Construct a locus of points that are the same distance from Hamilton and Navier.

● Navier

Hamilton ●

**12**

44 cats and 46 dogs are admitted to a veterinary hospital in one week.

50 of these animals are vaccinated.

Four times as many cats as dogs are not vaccinated.

Complete the frequency tree.

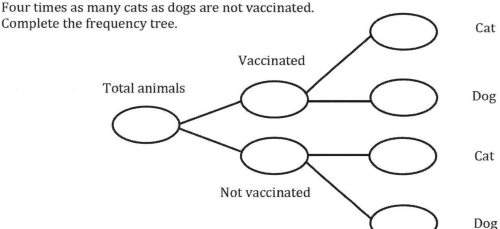

**13**

A new light bulb reduces energy consumption by 35%.

The new light bulb consumes 7.93 units of energy.

What was the energy consumption before the new light bulb?

**14**

The distance from Norwich to Nuneaton is 144 miles.

A bus travels from Norwich to Nuneaton setting off at 2:15pm.

The bus travels at an average speed of 40mph.

When does the bus arrive in Nuneaton?

**15**

A car travels 120 miles at 48 mph and then a further 80 miles at 50mph.

If instead the car travelled the whole distance at a speed of 49mph, how would this affect the travel time?

You must show your working.

**16**

Here is some data on the length of time doctors worked in a hospital.

- Shortest time 90 minutes
- Longest time 15 hours
- Median time 12 hours
- Upper quartile 13 hours
- Interquartile range 4 hours

Complete the box plot below to show the data.

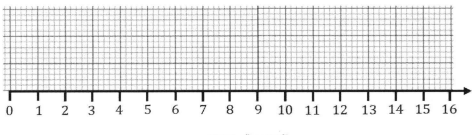

Time (hours)

**17**

In the Venn diagram
$\xi$ represents 43 people in a restaurant.
$S$ is people who had a starter.
$D$ is people who had a dessert.
One person is picked at random.
Work out the probability this person had a dessert.

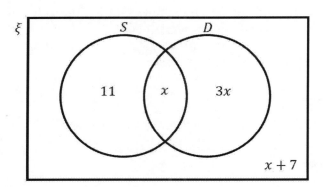

**18**

In the Venn diagram
$\xi$ represents 39 people who travel to work.
$C$ is people who travel by car.
$T$ is people who travel by train.
One person who travels by train is picked at random.
Work out the probability this person also travels by car.

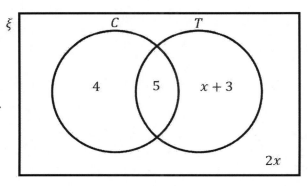

**19**

Find the highest common factor (HCF) of $12x^2y^3$ and $24xy^2$

**20**

$f(x) = x^3 - x^2$
Find the value of $f(-2)$

**21**

A supermarket sells loaves of bread.
The store manager has a stocklist of three types of bread.
brown : white : wholemeal $= 7 : 11 : 3$
There are 3236 more brown loaves than wholemeal loaves.
How many white loaves are on the stocklist?

**22**

Expand and simplify $(5x^2 + 3)(2x - 3) - 10x(x^2 - 4)$

**23**

$A, B$ and $C$ are points on the circumference of the circle.
$CP$ is a tangent.
Write down the size of angle $x$.

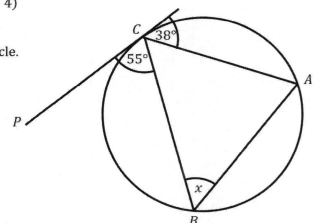

**24**

$a$ is a positive number.
$b$ is 20% more than $a$.
$c$ is 20% less than $b$.
Rectangle P has sides $a$ and $b$.
Rectangle Q has sides $a$ and $c$.
Rectangle R has sides $b$ and $c$.
Which rectangle has the greatest area?

**25**

$M$ is a number written as a product of its prime factors:  $M = 2^3 \times 3^2 \times 5^4$
$N$ is a number written as a product of its prime factors:  $N = 2^2 \times 3 \times 5^4$
Write the number $N + M$ as a product of its prime factors.

**26**

$ABC$ is a triangle.
Calculate the length of $AB$.

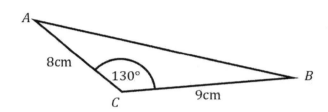

**27**

A graph is drawn to represent the region $R$ by the three inequalities shown.

$$x + y < 5 \qquad y < 3 \qquad y \geq x + 1$$

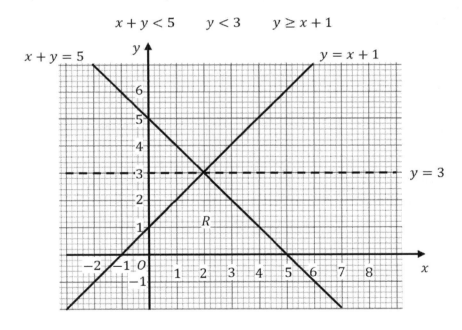

Analyse the graph and comment on any errors.

**28**

$p : q = 7 : 3$
$8q = 11r$
Find the ratio $p : r$ in its simplest form.

**29**

The temperature of a pan of hot water is decreasing.
The graph shows the temperature of the pan over two hours.
Estimate the rate of decrease in temperature at 30 minutes.

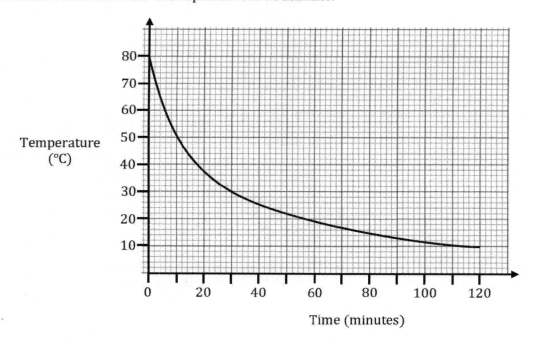

**30**

**(a)**

$a$ and $b$ are positive integers.
Prove that $a^2 + 2ab + b^2$ is a square number.

**(b)**

$ab = 42$ and $a + b = 13$

Find the value of $\dfrac{1}{a} + \dfrac{1}{b}$

**31**

$ABCDE$ is a square-based pyramid.
The height of the pyramid is twice the length $AB$.
The volume of the pyramid is 1152cm³.

Volume of pyramid $= \dfrac{1}{3} \times$ base area $\times$ height

Find the length $AC$.

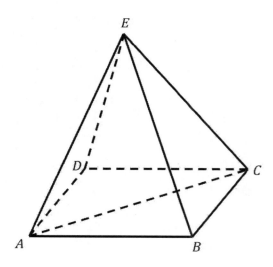

**32**

A population $P$ of ants are modelled by the formula below.

$P = A \times t^{b-2}$

$A$ is a constant.

$t$ is the time in days.

When $P = 4000, b = 2$

When $P = 9600, b = 3$

Find the value of $P$ when $b = 5$

**33**

The graph of a quadratic function $y = g(x)$ is shown below.

Write down the range of values for $x$ for which $g(x) > 0$

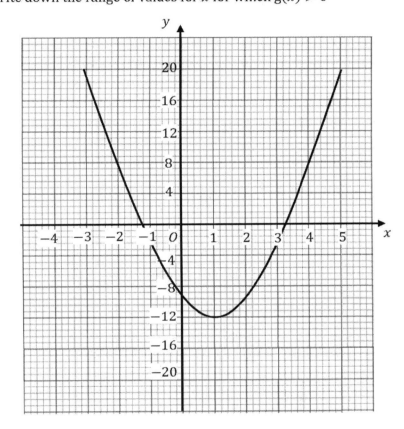

**34**

$f(x) = \dfrac{x}{6} - 3$

$g(x) = 12x^2 + 18$

Find $fg(x)$ in fully simplified form.

## Paper 3 Higher: Practice Set 2 Solutions

**1**

A solid circle means $x$ can be equal to the value.
A hollow circle means $x$ cannot be equal to the value.
The correct inequality is $-4 \leq x < 10$

**2**

200% more means twice the original value is added to the original value.
The new value obtained would be 300% of its original.
The correct ratio is $x : y = 1 : 3$

**3**

The sequence increases by 6 each time: the first part of the $n$th term is $6n$.
Subtract the difference (6) from the first term ($-8$) to obtain $-14$.
Combine these two terms to obtain the $n$th term: $6n - 14$

**4**

Any equation of the form $y = a$ will be parallel to the $x$-axis.
The correct answer is $y = -0.5$

**5**

$$(x - 12)^2 = (x - 12)(x - 12)$$
$$= x^2 - 12x - 12x + 144$$
$$= x^2 - 24x + 144$$

**6**

$$561 = 512 + 49$$
$$= 8^3 + 7^2$$

Any pairing of $8^3$ and $7^2$ is acceptable.

**7**

There are 60 films.
The median will be at the halfway mark (30).
Find the cumulative frequency of each of the given intervals.
The first interval that has a cumulative total greater than or equal to 30 will contain the median.

| Time, $t$ minutes | Number of films | Cumulative frequency |
|---|---|---|
| $60 < t \leq 90$ | 7 | 7 |
| $90 < t \leq 110$ | 15 | 22 |
| $110 < t \leq 140$ | 13 | 35 |
| $140 < t \leq 180$ | 25 | 60 |

The $110 < t \leq 140$ interval has a cumulative total of 35, therefore the median is in this interval.

**8**

Metric units are metres (m), kilograms (kg) or litres (L).
They typically have units that come in multiples of 10s such as:
100cm in 1m or 1000g in 1kg.
Length and perimeter are one dimensional and measured in metres.
Area is two dimensional so has a square: $m^2$
Volume is three dimensional so has a cube: $m^3$

| Length | Area | Volume | Perimeter |
|---|---|---|---|
| m | $m^2$ | $m^3$ | m |

**9**

$$s = 0.5(u + v)t$$
$$2s = (u + v)t \qquad \text{Multiply by 2.}$$
$$\frac{2s}{t} = u + v \qquad \text{Divide by } t.$$
$$\qquad\qquad\qquad \text{Subtract } u.$$
$$v = \frac{2s}{t} - u$$

**10**

Angle $CBD$ is alternate to angle $BDE$: so, angle $BDE = 2x$
Triangle $EBD$ is isosceles: so, angle $BED = 2x$
Opposite angles in a parallelogram are equal:
$$3x = 2x + 22$$
$$x = 22$$

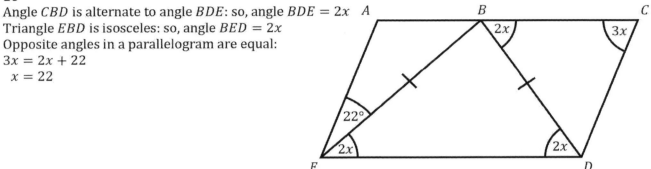

**11**

Hamilton and Navier are two points.
The locus of points equidistant from two points is the perpendicular bisector of the line joining the two points.

Set the compass length equal to the distance between Hamilton and Navier.

Draw an arc centred on Navier.

Draw an arc centred on Hamilton ensuring that this arc crosses the first arc.

Join the points of intersection with a ruler to produce the locus of points required.

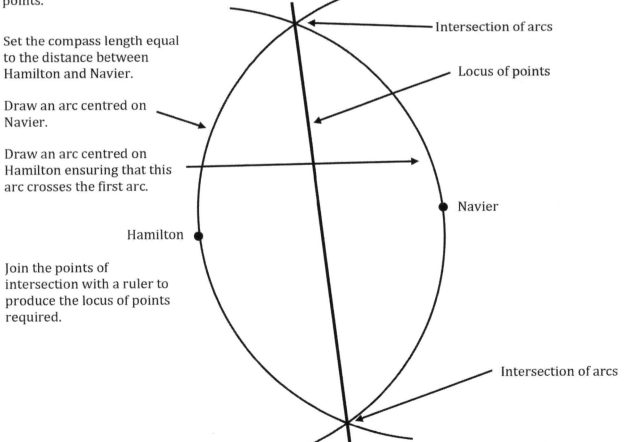

**12**

$44 + 46 = 90$ so the total number of animals is 90.

There were 50 vaccinated animals, meaning the remaining 40 were unvaccinated.

The ratio of unvaccinated cats to unvaccinated dogs is 4 : 1

This ratio is dividing the 40 unvaccinated animals.

40 divided 4 : 1 is 32 : 8

There were 32 unvaccinated cats and 8 unvaccinated dogs.

There are 44 cats altogether so 12 cats are vaccinated.

There are 46 dogs altogether so 38 dogs are vaccinated.

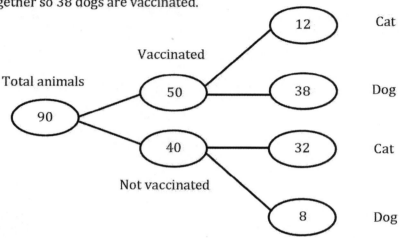

**13**

The multiplier to reduce by 35% is 0.65

The original energy consumption was multiplied by 0.65 to give 7.93:

$$\text{energy consumption before} \times 0.65 = 7.93$$
$$\text{energy consumption before} = \frac{7.93}{0.65}$$
$$= 12.2$$

The energy consumption before was 12.2 units.

**14**

$$\text{time} = \frac{\text{distance}}{\text{speed}}$$
$$= \frac{144}{40}$$
$$= 3.6 \text{ hours}$$

Convert 0.6 hours into minutes: $0.6 \times 60 = 36$ minutes.

The bus travelled for 3 hours and 36 minutes.

The bus set off at 2:15pm which means it arrived at 5:51pm.

**15**

The travel time will be reduced if the average speed is increased.

The journey is split into two parts:

$$\text{time} = \frac{\text{distance}}{\text{speed}} \qquad \text{time} = \frac{\text{distance}}{\text{speed}}$$
$$= \frac{120}{48} \qquad\qquad = \frac{80}{50}$$
$$= 2.5 \text{ hours} \qquad = 1.6 \text{ hours}$$

The total time for the journey is $2.5 + 1.6 = 4.1$ hours.

The mean speed for the original journey is:

$$speed = \frac{distance}{time}$$

$$= \frac{120 + 80}{4.1}$$

$$= 48.78 \dots mph$$

If the car travelled at 49mph then the journey would be completed in less time.

## 16

Five values are required to draw a box plot:

Minimum, lower quartile, median, upper quartile and maximum.

The lower quartile is the difference between the upper quartile and interquartile range:

$$lower\ quartile = upper\ quartile - interquartile\ range$$

$$= 13 - 4$$

$$= 9$$

The shortest time, 90 minutes, is 1.5 hours.

The completed box plot is shown below.

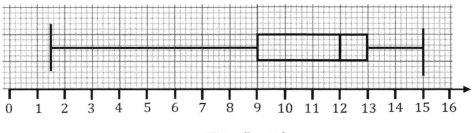

Time (hours)

## 17

The sum of all the entries in the Venn diagram is 43:

$$11 + x + 3x + x + 7 = 43$$

$$5x + 18 = 43$$

$$5x = 25$$

$$x = 5$$

Number of people who had dessert $= 4x$

$$= 20$$

Probability of selecting a person who had dessert $= \dfrac{20}{43}$

## 18

The sum of all the entries in the Venn diagram is 39:

$$4 + 5 + x + 3 + 2x = 39$$

$$3x + 12 = 39$$

$$3x = 27$$

$$x = 9$$

Number of people who travel by train $= 5 + x + 3$

$$= 17$$

Probability of selecting a person who travelled by car given they travelled by train $= \dfrac{5}{17}$

## 19

The highest common factor is the largest factor of two or more numbers.

In the case of algebraic expressions, the highest common factor is the highest power of a term that is a factor of both expressions.

The HCF of $12x^2y^3$ and $24xy^2$ is $12xy^2$

## 20

$$f(x) = x^3 - x^2$$
$$f(-2) = (-2)^3 - (-2)^2$$
$$= -8 - 4$$
$$= -12$$

## 21

The difference between brown and wholemeal is 3236.
This difference in the ratio is 4, from $7 - 3 = 4$
4 parts of this ratio are equal to 3236.
The number of white loaves is 11 parts.
no. of white loaves $= \dfrac{3236}{4} \times 11 = 8899$
There are 8899 white loaves on the stocklist.

## 22

$$(5x^2 + 3)(2x - 3) - 10x(x^2 - 4) = 10x^3 - 15x^2 + 6x - 9 - 10x^3 + 40x$$
$$= -15x^2 + 46x - 9$$

## 23

Using the alternate segment theorem: $x = 38°$

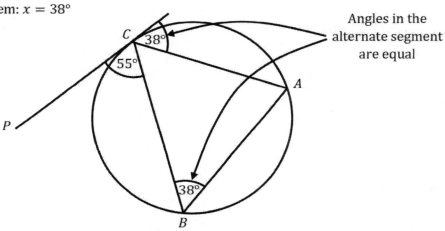

Angles in the alternate segment are equal

## 24

$b$ is 20% more than $a$: $b = 1.2a$
$c$ is 20% less than $b$: $c = 0.8b$
The areas of each rectangle, in terms of $a$:

Area of P $= ab$
$= a(1.2a)$
$= 1.2a^2$

Area of Q $= ac$
$= a(0.8b)$
$= 0.8a(1.2a)$
$= 0.96a^2$

Area of R $= bc$
$= (1.2a)(0.8b)$
$= 0.96a(1.2a)$
$= 1.152a^2$

Rectangle P has the greatest area.

## 25

For the working, factor out the common factors of $N$ and $M$ then simplify:
$$N + M = 2^2 \times 3 \times 5^4 + 2^3 \times 3^2 \times 5^4$$
$$= (2^2 \times 3 \times 5^4)(1 + 2 \times 3)$$
$$= (2^2 \times 3 \times 5^4)(7)$$
$$= 2^2 \times 3 \times 5^4 \times 7$$

**26**
Using the cosine rule (indicated by the angle-sandwich of 130° between 8 and 9):

$a^2 = b^2 + c^2 - 2bc \cos A$
$AB^2 = AC^2 + CB^2 - 2(AC)(CB) \cos 130°$
$\quad = 8^2 + 9^2 - 2 \times 8 \times 9 \cos 130°$
$\quad = 237.56 ...$
$AB = 15.413 ...$

The length $AB$ is 15.4cm (3sf).

**27**
$x + y < 5$ should be a dashed line not solid.
$R$ should be on the other side of $y \geq x + 1$
The correct diagram is shown below.

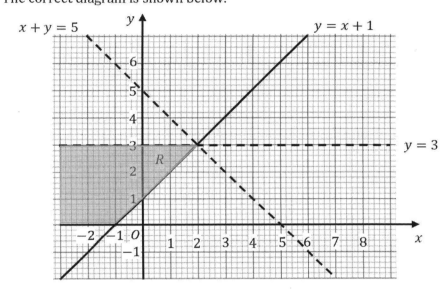

For $y \geq x + 1$ use the origin test to establish which side of the line is required. The origin has coordinates (0,0), so:

$y \geq x + 1$
$0 \geq 0 + 1$ which is not true. This means that $R$ goes on the side that does not contain the origin.

**28**
$p : q = 7 : 3$
Use ratio cross multiply to find an equation for $p$ and $q$:
$7q = 3p$
$q = \dfrac{3}{7}p$ [1]

Substitute the value of $q$ found in [1] into the equation $8q = 11r$

$8\left(\dfrac{3}{7}p\right) = 11r$
$\dfrac{24}{7}p = 11r$
$24p = 77r$

Use ratio cross multiply to find $p : r$
$p : r = 77 : 24$

$p : q$

$7 : 3$
$7q = 3p$

$24p = 77r$

$p : r$
$77 : 24$

**29**
The rate of decrease at 30 minutes is the gradient of the curve when the time is 30 minutes.
Questions that use "rate" in association with a graph usually mean calculate the gradient.
Approximate a gradient using a ruler when the time is 30 minutes.
Extend the gradient line until it intersects the $x$ and $y$ axes.
This makes the calculation of the gradient easier.

$$\text{gradient} = \frac{\text{vertical length}}{\text{horizontal length}}$$
$$= \frac{46}{86}$$
$$= 0.53$$

The rate of decrease of temperature when the time is 30 minutes is approximately 0.53°C/min.
Any answer of the form $0.53 \pm 0.03$ will be acceptable.

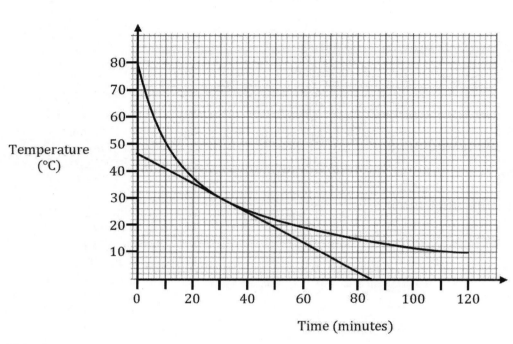

## 30(a)

The question is testing knowledge of the general expansion of a two-term expression when squared.
$$a^2 + 2ab + b^2 = (a + b)(a + b)$$
$$= (a + b)^2$$

Since $a$ and $b$ are integers $(a + b)$ is an integer and $(a + b)^2$ is a square number.

## 30(b)

Two methods can be used here:

Method 1: find a common denominator.
$$\frac{1}{a} + \frac{1}{b} = \frac{a + b}{ab}$$
$$= \frac{13}{42}$$

Method 2: solve simultaneous equations using a substitution.
$$a = \frac{42}{b}, \quad \text{substitute into } a + b = 13$$
$$\frac{42}{b} + b = 13$$
$$42 + b^2 = 13b$$
$$b^2 - 13b + 42 = 0$$
$$(b - 6)(b - 7) = 0$$
$$b = 6 \text{ or } b = 7$$

Substituting either value in $a + b = 13$ means $a = 6$ when $b = 7$ or $a = 7$ when $b = 6$
$$\frac{1}{a} + \frac{1}{b} = \frac{1}{6} + \frac{1}{7}$$
$$= \frac{13}{42}$$

**31**

Let $AB = x$ ; then the height of the pyramid is $2x$

$BC = x$ since the base is a square.

Substitute the values into the volume equation and solve for $x$:

$\frac{1}{3} \times$ base area $\times$ height $=$ Volume of pyramid

$$\frac{1}{3} \times x^2 \times 2x = 1152$$

$$\frac{2}{3} x^3 = 1152$$

$$x^3 = 1728$$

$$x = 12$$

$ABC$ is a right-angled triangle so Pythagoras can be used to find $AC$:

$$AC^2 = AB^2 + BC^2$$
$$= 12^2 + 12^2$$
$$= 288$$
$$AC = 12\sqrt{2}$$
$AC = 12\sqrt{2}$ or 16.97cm (2dp)

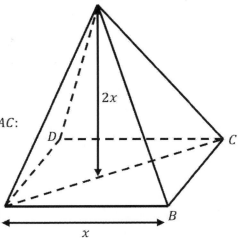

**32**

Substitute each of the given conditions into the formula to find $A$ and $t$:

$P = A \times t^{b-2}$

$4000 = A \times t^{2-2}$      When $P = 4000, b = 2$

$4000 = A \times 1$

$A = 4000$

$P = 4000 \times t^{b-2}$

$9600 = 4000 \times t^{3-2}$      When $P = 9600, b = 3$

$9600 = 4000t$

$t = 2.4$

$P = 4000 \times 2.4^{b-2}$

Now substitute $b = 5$ into the equation to find $P$:

$P = 4000 \times 2.4^{5-2}$

$= 55296$

The ant population when $b = 5$ is 55296.

**33**

$g(x) > 0$ is defined when the curve is above the $x$-axis.

This is defined by the inequalities $x < -1.2$ and $x > 3.2$

Note that if the question uses a symbol $>$ or $<$ the answer cannot contain $\geq$ or $\leq$

**34**

$$\text{fg}(x) = \text{f}\big(\text{g}(x)\big)$$
$$= \text{f}(12x^2 + 18)$$
$$= \frac{12x^2 + 18}{6} - 3$$
$$= 2x^2 + 3 - 3$$
$$= 2x^2$$

## ABOUT THE AUTHOR

Barton Maths Tuition provides educational texts for GCSE students. The author is a private maths and science tutor supporting students in the area around Barton Under Needwood, Staffordshire.

Printed in Great Britain
by Amazon

30203267R00059